Contents

List of figures, tables and boxes

Figures

Tables

Boxes

Preface

At the end of *The purpose of planning*[1] I suggested that there were three main take-home messages. The first highlighted that change in the built environment is driven by the dynamics of private sector development markets and that the role and outcomes of planning processes need to be seen in the context of such economic dynamics. The second was that public engagement is difficult for structural as well as political reasons and not always likely to meet the promises and expectations of practitioners and theorists. And the third was that planning needs to be about achieving a better environment for people to live in and, because of the inevitable tensions between public and private interests, the focus in planning debates needs to move away from an emphasis on process to consideration of such substantive matters. Sustainability was evoked as a good measure of such an improved living environment, with its emphasis on livelihood, quality of life and environmental protection of well-being.

The conclusion considered – quite briefly – how livelihood, quality of life and well-being might differ under a more sustainable future, and specifically considered the possibility that this future would have to be a lower growth one. It used the insights of Tim Jackson's book *Prosperity without growth*[2] to suggest what that future might look like – a heavier emphasis on services rather than production and consumption of material goods, better protection of environments and ecosystems and a focus on happiness and well-being rather than the pursuit of GDP (gross domestic product, the common measure of economic growth).

The book was completed before the financial crises of 2008 onwards precipitated us into a recession. This new book takes up some of the themes of *The purpose of planning* and reconsiders them in the light of current and future low economic growth, looking in more detail at how urban change can occur without the engine of growth and the driving involvement of private development markets. It spells out the reforms that will be needed if the planning system is to play a positive role in supporting people's well-being under these conditions, suggesting specific shifts in national planning policy guidance, different emphases in local planning and a renewed attention to how planning regulation works. It also considers the new demands on community engagement that this suggests.

This is not an introduction to the current planning system and how it works but rather an intervention in debates about what the planning system should be doing, the role it should play and how it should work. It is hoped that – in the spirit of debate – there will be disagreement as well as agreement with the arguments put forward here. To this end, a dedicated blog – 'Beyond Growth Dependent Planning' at http://beyondgrowthdependentplanning.blogspot. co.uk – has been opened to take this debate forward. You are warmly invited to join in.

I am extremely grateful to Julian Agyeman, Tim Marshall and Andy Thornley for generously giving of their time to comment on earlier drafts. They were a great help to me in sharpening the argument, even when they disagreed! Thanks also to Emily Watt and her team at Policy Press for being so collaborative, helpful, efficient and understanding.

Yvonne Rydin

ONE

Introducing growth-dependent planning

Welcome to Anywheretown – the home of growth dependence!

Five years ago the town centre of Anywheretown could only be described as run-down. There were boarded-up shop fronts in the high street and charity shops abounded. In the small 1970s shopping mall, the wind whistled through the bleak empty space collecting litter around the benches and the concrete planters. People complained of the lack of shopping opportunities and the need to travel to the nearest city for most of the big multiples like Marks & Spencer or Top Shop. A number of unemployed young people hung around, some drinking. There were some light industry and distribution companies in the estates on the outskirts of the town and a mix of services in the few office blocks by the station and in the myriad small spaces on the floors above shops. However, employment opportunities were tight and did not seem to be growing.

Fast forward a few years and the town seems transformed. Spotting the benefits of the soon-to-be improved rail links into Anycity, a developer bought up some land between the station and the town centre that previously housed a car park, some industrial sheds and a car repair works. This has been redeveloped into a new office complex with direct links to the station but also, through a new thoroughfare, to the town centre. This has shifted the retail centre of the town to the shopping mall, which has been refurbished and partially closed to the weather. The bright, warm interior has now attracted those elusive multiples, with the all-important Marks & Spencer located just where the footfall between the station and the town centre is most intense. The townscape has benefited from considerable landscaping improvements, paid for by the developers. Cafés have moved into the open air section of the old shopping mall and put their tables outside under the new trees. New parking has been provided for the additional shoppers and office workers but also bicycle racks and lighting and distinctive paving for pedestrian routes into the town centre.

This is a success story and it is not the intention of this book to argue that such urban change should be resisted or critiqued wholesale. Such market-led redevelopment can contribute to regeneration of our urban areas and to the improvement of the built environment and people's quality of life. However, it is not and cannot be the recipe for everywhere and everyone at all times.

For a long time, the planners for Anywheretown were unable to attract any new development of any scale in the town centre. Development briefs were drawn up and circulated but interest by developers was sporadic and did not come to fruition. It took a particular developer to notice the potential offered by the proposed rail improvements into a city that was itself experiencing buoyant market conditions. The developer calculated the risk of the project they were proposing as acceptable to themselves and their funders and was willing to sit down and discuss urban and building design issues with the planners. The result was broadly acceptable to the developer, the local authority and the more vocal elements of the local community.

However, not everyone is completely happy. Retailers at the further end of the old high street have seen trade sucked away from their locations and into the refurbished shopping mall. The growth in commuter traffic has lifted local house prices and encouraged some new residential development. But the cost of this housing is beyond the reach of many local households, going instead to people from Anycity. This local population growth has provided even further footfall into the new shopping centre but done little to rejuvenate the light industrial estates on the town's outskirts. Areas of lower-income housing on the town's periphery are home to substantial numbers of households where at least one member is out of work and money is tight. The Marks & Spencer in the town centre is irrelevant to their shopping needs.

This form of planning is described here as *growth-dependent planning*. The essence of such planning is the reliance on private sector development to generate benefits for the wider community and the use of the planning system to achieve this. It is the argument of this book, that over the last 40 years, the British planning system has become dominated by the paradigm of growth-dependent planning. It further argues that there are a number of reasons why this paradigm is no longer – if it ever has been – appropriate as the sole framework for guiding planning practice. Looking at the economic dimensions suggests that it is largely irrelevant for many locations at many times. Growth cannot be relied on to drive urban change across the country, particularly in the current economic crisis. This is doubly so if the constraints on public sector expenditure under an austerity-framed fiscal policy are taken into account. But beyond these economic arguments, there are serious concerns about the social impact of growth-dependent planning in certain locations and the way that it encourages, is even defined by, the replacement of low land values with higher values and associated change in land uses and communities. Finally, there are some doubts as to the environmental sustainability of a growth-dependent paradigm, despite the claims that are made for green growth and new green urban development.

By why should this paradigm of planning have come to dominate policy and practice? The answer can be found in the emergence of governance modes of governing and the specific response of normative planning theorising known as collaborative planning. This is explored next.

Governance: the context for growth dependence

There is a broader context for this emphasis on growth dependence within the British planning system. This relates to an important shift in the late 20th century from 'government' to 'governance' as an account of how the state governs. Throughout the 1990s and into the early 21st century, governance theories were developed to understand the change that was occurring in a range of public sector activities – including planning – at both central and local levels.[1]

Drawing on experience in the US as well as the UK, governance describes a situation where the ability to implement government strategy, the 'capacity to act' as Stone puts it,[2] is dependent not on state action alone but also on bringing together a range of stakeholders to pool their resources, knowledge and decision-making powers. This is contrasted to the more hierarchical approach of 'government' which sees the state as uniquely powerful, holding considerable resources and in control of the direction of change in society. The power of the state using processes of direct 'government' has increasingly been recognised as limited in practice. The ability to govern has been seen as constrained by the need to garner legitimacy within society more generally and to harness resources, many of which are held by actors outside of the state. Therefore the era of 'government' has been replaced by that of 'governance', in which both policy formulation and, importantly, policy implementation, are shared among a range of actors.

Within governance theories, the emphasis has been on looking at the interrelationships between multiple actors across the state, the private sector and civil society, and how these have an impact on policy outcomes. The argument has been that governance processes of complex interrelationships within partnerships and networks of various kinds can be more effective than direct government action through the ability to leverage information and other resources, including finance. Some argue, with reason, that such governance is still occurring 'in the shadow' of government, of continuing hierarchical relationships between the state, on the one hand, and the private sector and civil society, on the other.[3] But even if one accepts (as one clearly should) that the state still exercises certain key hierarchical powers, this does not deny the insights offered by the governance literature. Government bodies, including local government, now spend much time within policy and planning processes, engaging with this wider range of stakeholders in order to achieve their ends, and this is actively promoted as 'good governance'.

This broader shift in how the state governs has provided the opportunity for growth dependence to become the accepted paradigm for planning. Governance approaches – in policy practice as well as academic theory – have provided the legitimacy for market actors to exercise power within relationships of governing given the widely-acknowledged insufficient capacity within the public sector to drive forward urban change on its own. In accordance with the ideology of governance, such market actors sit alongside other actors from other sectors (public, private, civil society). The aim is a win-win outcome, agreement and compromise to the mutual satisfaction of all involved. But it needs to be remembered that the reason for market actors being invited into policy formulation and implementation is because they hold certain resources – particularly financial resources – that the public sector does not. This creates a structural imbalance within governance processes and gives the promotion of market-led economic activity a certain prominence. Hence governance processes offer the opportunity for embedding growth dependence within the planning system. The detail of how this occurred, up to and including the present day, is covered in the next chapter.

Within the discipline of planning, a specific body of normative planning theory has provided conceptual support for adopting governance approaches to planning practice.[4] In response to the growing recognition of the limited ability of planners to effect change on their own and the need to engage with others in the private sector and also in civil society, planning theory developed a distinctive new approach during the latter part of the 20th century. This approach – generally termed collaborative planning – also addressed criticisms that had been levelled at planners for failing to consult and work with local communities on changes affecting their local areas, and recognised the extent to which changes in the built environment had not met communities' expectations and needs. It sought to bring together interests and stakeholders across the boundaries of the public and private sectors, across the silos of specific departments and organisations and across scales from the local communities to the service and infrastructure providers operating within a broader area. The aim was the widest involvement of those involved in progressing urban change or affected by such change in plan making for a locality.

Collaborative planning draws on the Habermasian concept of communicative action and seeks to recast planning practice in terms of engagement between key stakeholders, emphasising the role that communication and dialogue play in shaping plan making, plans and subsequent decisions.[5] While the considerable literature on this approach does discuss the impact of power relations and inequalities between different stakeholders, the core of the approach, as it has been widely interpreted, is the potential for agreement and even consensus to arise from communication between actors.[6] For this to be achieved, however, the communication needs to be genuine, based on a full appreciation by stakeholders of their own interests and undertaken with the aim of mutual understanding between parties. Innes and Booher talk of the 'network power' operating through such communication as being able, to some extent, to overcome other structural power relationships between actors.[7]

There has been considerable debate about the effectiveness of such collaborative planning in practice.[8] The ideal speech situation – in which mutual understanding and consensus can be achieved by all participants – rarely actually exists. Therefore planners are faced with negotiating existing relationships of power when they produce plans, projects and decisions. The resource imbalance between market actors and others, noted above, creates an inequitable baseline with regard to such negotiations. Developers can always exercise an investment strike and withdraw from activity in a locality if they are not happy with the negotiation outcomes;[9] planners and communities, on their side, have the resources of regulatory power to negotiate side-benefits from developments but they are not able to force the development to go ahead. As will be explored in Chapters 3 and 4, in some circumstances, planning authorities can invest in infrastructure, subsidise land purchases or otherwise create more attractive contexts for the market-led development. But the extent of public sector resources available for these activities is highly constrained; this is the important context for the emergence of growth-dependent planning in the first place.

Furthermore, planners' expertise and the adequacy of the training they receive to redress these power imbalances through communicative action within planning situations have been questioned.[10] Calls are only now being made for planners to develop proper mediation skills which are but a stepping stone on the way to the full communicative engagement envisaged by collaborative planning.[11] This particularly affects the way in which local communities and groups within those communities are able to engage in the planning discussions affecting their localities. The distinction between consultation, participation and full engagement in planning processes has been repeatedly identified by academics and practitioners, together with the tendency for planning practices to stop at consultation rather than look for any deeper involvement of communities with plan making and development projects.[12] In particular, lower-income communities have been repeatedly let down by conventional consultation exercises. Their lack of purchasing power within the marketplace means that their arguments about urban development have less force and they are rarely able to challenge the logic of a growth-dependent planning proposal.

Of course, community and environmental interests may not always wish to resist this logic. There will be circumstances where the prospects of market-led development offer opportunities for improving everyday life and contributing to sustainable development. The prospects of planning gain – community benefits provided by the developer – can be significant in persuading local communities of the value of such a proposal. There are possibilities, as in the London Borough of Southwark, for local communities to store up examples of planning gain they would like to see provided by developers.[13] The environmental sustainability credentials of a new development project may be considerable and convincing as with zero-carbon or passive house standard development.[14] In making the argument for an alternative to the paradigm of growth-dependent planning, it is important to recognise that this paradigm can be effective in creating a form of urban change that is market-led but also planning-shaped and that does deliver environmental and social benefits alongside economic activity and profit.

Innes and Booher have identified the circumstances in which collaborative approaches are able to deliver in the broader public interest even while reliant on powerful economic actors for key investments.[15] They point out that these approaches only work when all actors recognise their interdependence; each party needs to recognise their mutual dependence on each other. Thus a development can provide the opportunity for community benefits *and* economic profit to be released by the combination of market-led economic activity and planning regulation supported by community involvement. However, this will only be the case up to a point, the limits of development viability as outlined in Chapter 3.

In other circumstances, the identification of mutual dependence may be much more difficult to achieve. Communities may just not want the development being offered by market actors. The extent of the planning gain may be insufficient to persuade them otherwise. Similarly, environmental concerns may be voiced that cannot be resolved by negotiation. In response, some have called instead for a planning approach that emphasises the centrality of conflict as opposed to the hope of consensus or compromise. Within such 'agonistic' planning theory, the focus is on how to empower the most vulnerable within society and ensure that they have equal status within planning practice to other stakeholders.[16]

But recognising conflict − while avoiding the illusion that collaborative planning is being pursued − may not be sufficient to produce outcomes that benefit these community and environmental interests at the expense of market actors, and it has to be at their expense if there is an actual conflict involved. Collaborative and related governance approaches will not work if market actors are not dependent on existing communities and environmental interest groups to achieve their development goals. Such dependence can only come from the planning authority exercising a strong framework of planning policy and regulation in support of such community and environmental interests but, as has been argued and will be developed in Chapter 3, this will be constrained by the possibility − at some point − of the developer deciding the project is not viable and walking away.

Planners thus often see little alternative to supporting market-led development, even at the cost of negative impacts on some of their local communities and environmental concerns, because otherwise the opportunity for urban change will disappear as the developer looks elsewhere for sites and more amenable local planning authorities. They have to make a judgement call − along with local politicians − on whether the development, taken as a whole, is the best prospect of change for the area. Some local people, groups and political representatives may argue that any development is undesirable, taking the NIMBY (Not In My Back Yard) route; but others will find themselves wanting urban change and development in the locality and having to take a view, a gamble, on whether the offered development is the best option available, whether any other developer will offer more or whether no development at all is to be preferred. This is often an invidious position for local communities, politicians and planners to find themselves in. But what is the alternative?

Alternative responses to growth dependence

Growth-dependent planning is never going to be able to achieve desirable change in all locations at all times and meet the needs of all groups in society. It has clearly delivered some benefits within Anywheretown, but there were times when this strategy did not work for Anywheretown, and there will be Othertowns elsewhere that have desperately tried the Anywheretown solution without success. What if we are in the midst – or to be more pessimistic, at the start – of a period when growth-dependent planning is just not going to work for most towns and cities? And it is clear that, while some are reaping benefits, there are also Anywheretown residents who are not getting any benefits from the new development and may even be feeling costs. This does not mean that the town centre redevelopment should not have gone ahead. We do not live in world of the economist's Pareto Optimum, that is where no change that benefits someone should go ahead unless no one else is hurt or everyone is adequately compensated for that hurt. Policy makers and planners often decide that a particular course of action benefits enough people to go ahead, regardless of the impact on another (hopefully smaller) group. But that does not mean these other residents of Anywheretown should be completely forgotten either.

What is to be done for the towns and cities, and the neighbourhoods within them, that cannot be reached by growth-dependent planning? What is the appropriate response? Three possible ways forward can be discerned.

First, it is possible to argue that there is no feasible alternative to growth-dependent planning. This approach would see market-led dynamics as the inevitably fundamental motor of economic and social life and due a degree of moral primacy as a result.[17] The way to deal with any problems arising from the dependence on growth is, therefore, to deregulate completely, to remove constraints on market development and to steer whatever public sector funds that are available towards the support of such private sector development. Negative social and environmental impacts would be seen as regrettable but unavoidable and, ultimately, forgettable in the pursuit of the assumed benefits of market-led development activity. It is doubtful if this is an ethical planning position. It certainly goes against the fundamental purpose of planning.

Second, it could be argued that the mistake is to rely on market-led actors to deliver urban change. Instead this reliance should be replaced with a stronger set of public sector activities.[18] This would look to macro-economic policies of Keynesianism to move the economy from low to higher growth and to use state investment in infrastructure and development of the built environment itself to shape the nature of urban change. It would look to macro policies to tackle the inequalities in society and achieve more sustainable pathways, and to public sector planning to ensure that all new developments met the needs of all groups in society and rigorous green standards. This would require a considerable political and ideological shift from the neoliberalism of the last few decades that has made this seem impracticable, costly and even economically destabilising.

Third – and this is the response that will be explored within this book – there is the possibility of moving away from a complete reliance on either a market-led or state-led approach and instead espousing community-based activity. The argument is that this will provide more sustainable pathways for urban development, pathways that are also able to meet the needs of lower-income and more vulnerable groups within society. This is a bottom-up approach that seeks to achieve societal change piecemeal. It suggests that a community-based approach may be appropriate for locations and situations where growth-dependent planning is not; it holds out the possibility of co-existence with growth-dependent planning operating in some locations and an alternative approach in others.

However, for this to be a possibility, the planning system needs to be reformed. The direction and detail of this reform is the subject of the second half of this book. Currently the institutional framework of the planning system embeds growth-dependent planning as the only alternative. Attention needs to be focused on the powers, incentives structures and prevailing norms within the planning system to understand how to give more scope for bottom-up action. For example, it will be argued later that regulation is currently not simply too weak but inappropriately structured to provide sufficient support for such action.

So it is argued that there is a need for a different kind of planning for the areas and people left behind by a dominance of the growth-dependent planning paradigm. The purpose of this book is to explore an alternative paradigm, to explain why it is necessary, and to consider how this different type of planning practice can co-exist with the continued successful experience of growth-dependent planning where and when it does work. It is not primarily about how growth-dependent planning can be made to work more effectively, equitably and sustainably. Some points of relevance to this problem are made along the way, but this is not the main purpose of this particular book.

The structure of the book

In the next chapter the case is made that growth dependence has become embedded in the planning system, and this is explained in detail with reference to the current institutions of planning in England. In Chapter 3 the key elements of the growth-dependent paradigm are set out, including the economic model underpinning this approach and the arguments made for its beneficial effects. Chapters 4 and 5 then develop a critique of this paradigm. Chapter 4 does this from an economic perspective, arguing that the economic conditions are not always favourable to a reliance on growth-dependent planning to deliver desired outcomes. Chapter 5 looks at the impact of the growth-dependent paradigm where social equity and the implications for environmental sustainability and environmental justice are concerned.

Chapter 6 begins the second half of the book by presenting an agenda for planning policy and practice that draws on concerns with well-being, environmental sustainability and environmental justice, framing this in terms of just sustainability. Chapters 7, 8 and 9 then discuss ways of delivering on this agenda using tools and approaches outside the growth-dependent paradigm. Chapter 7 looks at alternative development models; Chapter 8 considers new ways of improving existing places and spaces; and Chapter 9 discusses community ownership and management of assets for community enjoyment and benefit. Chapter 10 then brings together the argument of the book, making a series of specific recommendations for reforming the planning system to avoid an over-reliance on growth dependence. It considers national policy guidance, local planning, regulatory reform and new forms of community engagement.

Much of the book is about unpacking the implications of planning practice that is so reliant on economic processes and signals and suggesting alternatives for consideration. Together these alternatives comprise a new paradigm that – in combination with growth-dependent planning – is better placed to deliver fair and sustainable urban environments. This will not be the dominant mode of planning either for use everywhere within every Anywheretown at all times. But it could help address some persistent problems that growth-dependent planning has not been able to resolve, and provide a new sense of purpose for the planning profession.

TWO

Embedding growth dependence in the planning system

The last chapter introduced the paradigm of growth-dependent planning in outline form and argued that the rise of governance had enabled this paradigm to become embedded in the planning system. This chapter explores this embedding process in more detail, looking briefly at the history of planning over the past four decades and considering key aspects of the contemporary institutions of planning. In setting up the discussion of how growth dependence became and remains embedded in the institutions of the planning system, it is helpful to clarify a little further what growth-dependent planning is and what it is not.

Planning debates have had a tendency to become entrenched in dichotomies, typically between pro- and anti-development positions or between pro- and anti-regulation positions. Thus accounts of planning often tell how planning policy and practice has emphasised the release of land for development or, alternatively, has constrained such land releases. Or it has told the history of planning in terms of shifts between more and less regulatory phases. In these accounts, the emphasis on regulation within the planning system often becomes elided with concerns about the attitude to releasing land for development. It is assumed that the existence of these regulatory powers, and the strong support for their use, will lead to the use of regulation to restrict the supply of development land.

But the identification of the paradigm of growth-dependent planning importantly separates out these two aspects of planning policy and practice: the attitude to releasing land for market-led development and the effective exercise of planning regulation. This is because, for growth-dependent planning to deliver on its promises it requires *both* a commitment to fostering market development *and* a commitment to using regulatory powers to deliver social and environmental benefits. These only come into tension when the scale of those social and environmental benefits threatens the viability of market development (as will be explained in Chapter 3). Table 2.1 illustrates this distinction between growth-dependent planning and a planning approach that is purely concerned with promoting market-led development, that is, a de-regulation perspective.

Table 2.1 has two axes: the extent to which market-led development is prioritised and promoted, on the one hand, and the focus within the planning system on getting social and environmental benefits from new development on the other. Growth-dependent planning uses promotion *and* regulation of market-led development to get such benefits; this contrasts with a purely deregulation approach that seeks to promote such development and leaves the resulting benefits and impacts to be decided by market processes. There is inevitably a spectrum within growth-dependent planning in terms of how rigorously regulation is pursued and, as will be shown, there has been movement along this spectrum over time with changing national governments. But there is still a conceptual distinction between a planning system that is growth-dependent and uses the powers of that system to deliver collectively-determined benefits, and an approach that pursues deregulation and, say, handles conflicts arising from market-led development as a matter of private property rights.

Table 2.1 also identifies NIMBYism as combining a negative attitude to market-led development with a lack of interest in using the planning system to deliver social and environmental benefits. This points to the importance of the involvement and voice of certain sections of local communities in shaping decisions about

Table 2.1: Clarifying the growth-dependent planning paradigm

	Market-led development promoted	Market-led development not prioritised
Focus on getting social and environmental benefits from development	Growth-dependent planning	???
No effort to get social and environmental benefits from development	Deregulation within planning	NIMBYism

urban development and change. In one sense, NIMBYism depends on a degree of regulatory control in order to have any possibility of resisting development pressures. But the key point here is that it is not interested in either the direct, consequential or side-benefits of development (see Chapter 3). It is, therefore, in polar opposition to growth-dependent planning.

More interestingly, this table also clarifies that there is a missing cell, where we do not yet understand how the planning system can deliver wider social and environmental benefits without a reliance on market-led development. But what if the goal is a commitment to using the planning system to deliver social and environmental benefits but – for a variety of reasons – it is considered undesirable or inappropriate to rely on market-led development to do so? This is the conundrum that the second half of this book seeks to address. The rest of this chapter explores how growth dependence has come to dominate planning thought and the possibility of this alternative approach – the missing cell in Table 2.1 – has, therefore, been overlooked. It also shows how growth-dependent planning has moved between more and less emphasis on using the full regulatory powers of the planning system.

Planners' growing dependence on growth

It is a central thesis of the book's argument that over the last three to four decades, planning as a purposeful state activity has become increasingly and more explicitly shaped by a dependence on growth. Before the early 1970s, there was a prevailing assumption that planning systems should be able to direct urban change through a mix of indicative plans, regulation, and also the powers of landownership, direct public sector development and substantial infrastructure investment.[1] The New Towns such as Stevenage and Milton Keynes are perhaps the key exemplars of this approach, but the comprehensive postwar redevelopment of both commercial town centres and residential areas of substandard housing and the major road-building programmes are all part of a planning approach that seemed to put the public sector planner centre-stage.

This was perhaps an illusion since private sector development activity, particularly in building homes and creating commercial centres, has always been a key element. Public sector landownership, infrastructure investment and some direct development (mainly in housing) has always gone alongside the activities of the private sector development industry. Discourses around planning, however, chose not to emphasise this but rather presented planning as an unproblematic means of achieving action in line with desired goals, seeing the professional planner as the expert driving the process and engaging with other actors on the public sector's terms.

This came under challenge for two intertwined economic and political reasons. On the economic front, the crisis of the early 1970s brought the postwar boom to an abrupt end. A property speculation bubble collapsed and the ensuing recession created new economic conditions.[2] The detail of these economic ups and downs will be further discussed in Chapter 4, but for now it is worth noting that the recession of the 1970s made it clear that the planning system required economic activity to have something to regulate, guide and plan for. Even with substantial public sector investment in the built environment, private sector development was still important as the driver of urban change, and the planning system was significantly engaged in steering this private sector activity. With declines in public sector investment – as occurred after the crisis of the early 1970s – the role of the private sector in driving development became more evident.

Alongside – and heavily influenced by – these economic shifts went changes in political ideology which moved the planner from an apparently powerful state actor directing change to a much less socially valued professional. In particular planners collectively bore much of the blame for the emerging deficiencies of the postwar wave of urban development.[3] This might be considered unfair given the reliance on private sector developers for the delivery of much urban change in the postwar period, but the positioning of planners as apparently important state actors driving change was inevitably going to imply some responsibility for outcomes. The result was a much more negative view of state planning, from both right-wing and left-wing critics.

Those on the left saw the problematic outcomes as arising from the failure of planners to involve or even consult local communities adequately on the changes affecting their areas. As a result a wide range of redevelopment schemes were not meeting communities' needs and desires. This criticism was particularly addressed at the new residential areas that had been built. The demolition of appalling housing, in some cases dating back to the 19th century, had often been followed by redevelopment along modernist lines.[4] The resulting flats – sometimes medium-rise, sometimes high-rise – were often disliked and found to be unsuitable for family living. Construction standards were sometimes poor and building design faults – such as persistent damp or even structural instability – were revealed over time. The open spaces were often poorly managed and became sites for parking and rubbish bins rather than amenity or recreation spaces. The housing on greenfield locations, while usually more traditional in urban form and design, faced other criticisms for car dependence and lack of community facilities. Some criticised the standard of construction and the design of these estates as well. And the new city centre developments such as the Bull Ring in Birmingham or, on a smaller scale, the pedestrianised centres of New Towns such as Stevenage did not escape criticism either. They were also considered to be overly car-dependent and soul-less in their scale and design.

This was matched by a critique from those on the right who saw the planning system as frustrating the private sector when it sought to promote new development, development which by definition would meet unmet needs because it was responding to market signals.[5] This was the rise of the anti-regulation discourse within planning debates that has remained influential to this day. Planners were delaying such development, imposing unnecessary restrictions on it and thereby stultifying much-needed change in the urban environment. Not only were people being denied the benefits of new development, this was having a negative impact on national and local economic growth. Thus planners were criticised for the time they took to process planning applications and also for the resources going into drawing up plans, plans that often lagged behind the actual pace of development in an area. These critics argued instead that the planning system should be providing certainty for market actors on where new development would be permitted and ensuring a steady flow of land with development permission.

Thus during the 1970s the planning profession was caught between critiques of inadequate engagement with and treatment of local communities, on the one hand, and unnecessary bureaucracy, associated regulatory delays and unreasonable requirements made of developers, on the other. By the end of the 1970s the election of a right-wing government, under Margaret Thatcher, meant that the central government view of planning was firmly in the latter camp. The result was a further shift in the balance of power between planning authorities and developers, cementing the tendency of the decade.

A number of measures reduced the scope of regulation and incorporated a presumption in favour of development into the planning system. This began with residential development and the guidance to local authorities contained in Circular 9/80.[6] But it then spread to other types of development, such as retailing, which was permitted in a wider range of locations, including on controversial out-of-town sites. Special Planning Zones and Enterprise Zones created specific spatial areas where planning regulation was relaxed in order to encourage private sector development and Urban Development Corporations used cheap land transfers and public sector investment in site decontamination and infrastructure to support the viability of private development as part of an urban regeneration strategy.[7]

This was perhaps the zenith of the deregulation emphasis within postwar planning and it resulted in a further significant diminution in the status and power of planners. Local authority planning departments were reduced in size and functions and in some cases plan making and building control were outsourced to private consultancies. During this period, it seemed as if the planning profession had little to do but facilitate what market actors wanted to do. However, the key elements of the planning system – plan making over the vast majority of the country and case-by-case consideration of planning applications – remained in place, and the system was charged with delivering improvements in quality of life alongside greater opportunity for economic activity.

Indeed, even before the change from a Conservative to a Labour government in 1997, the replacement of Margaret Thatcher as Prime Minister by John Major in 1990 saw a shift in policy approach and the pendulum swinging back towards a more positive and even proactive role for the profession. The 1990 Town and Country Planning Act (through Section 70(2)) saw the return to a plan-led system rather than the reliance on a presumption in favour of development, and more emphasis was placed on the role of plans in deciding where development should occur. With a greater appreciation of the climate change agenda,[8] the negative impacts of allowing further growth in car use and the importance of the pattern of land uses in driving this growth, there was a change of policy on retail development. Out-of-town retailing was discouraged and a sequential test for retail development introduced in 1996, favouring inner-city sites before edge-of-town and then the out-of-site locations.[9]

With the advent of the New Labour government under Tony Blair, however, the growth-dependent paradigm for planning was most clearly expressed. The Blair government propounded a much more positive view of the role of planners, both in terms of influencing the spatial patterning of new development and in creating urban spaces that could meet the needs and desires of local communities. The latter ambition was framed in terms of a design-led urban renaissance (whereas the previous government had discouraged planners from getting too involved in decisions about design). The focus of this urban renaissance was on (re)designing the urban public realm so as to foster greater social interaction and pedestrian presence on streets and also in parks, squares and piazzas.[10] The aim was both greater environmental sustainability, in terms of a shift from cars to other modes of transport (walking and cycling), and also greater cohesion within society more generally. This agenda had some significant impact both in landmark projects such as the Liverpool Dockside, Victoria Gardens in Manchester and Trafalgar Square in London, and also in smaller, more routine development projects. The assumption was that urban areas and urban development could be planned to bring people into a shared public realm. Cultural venues were used as trigger developments within such urban renaissance strategies. Every city, and increasingly towns also, wanted an art gallery or museum such as the Gehry-designed Guggenheim in Bilbao to attract people into their newly designed urban realm. The Turner Gallery in Margate and the Hepworth Gallery in Wakefield are two of the latest examples of this trend.

And beyond this urban design and regeneration role for planning, New Labour looked to planners to redress some of the imbalance in development pressures across the country. However, they sought to do so without restricting growth in the Greater London region, which was seen as the engine of the national economy. The Sustainable Communities Plan of 2003 set out this strategy with a view to influencing local authorities' development plans.[11] There were two strands in this plan. On the one hand, four growth areas were identified – all in the southern part of England – where new development was to be encouraged and planned for. On the other hand, Housing Market Renewal Areas were identified as the strategy for more northern parts. Local housing markets exhibiting depressed prices and a high level of vacancies were so designated and, while there was funding for a range of area improvements, the main approach was to demolish housing with selective redevelopment to create a better balanced housing market in terms of supply and demand.

At the same time, New Labour sought to provide a greater voice within planning debates for community representatives through a variety of initiatives including a New Deal for Communities, the work of a Social Exclusion Unit, reframing the key local authority strategy as a Community Strategy and requiring community involvement to be an up-front and well-thought-through element of local planning.

While such New Labour planning marked a move away from the deregulation of the Thatcher years, it shared the belief that promoting market-led development was important for macro-economic reasons, and rather sought to use that development more fully for social and environmental benefit. This was still a long way from the postwar model of comprehensive planning based on public sector-led city centre redevelopment and council housebuilding. And it is still a long way from the model that operates in many other countries where local authority landownership and the ability to raise finance for infrastructure and other development puts local planners in a quite different relationship to market processes.[12] In the UK, while there have been shifts in emphasis in terms of a more or less positive view of the planning system and more or less pro-active use of planning regulation, since the 1970s the emphasis has been on creating the conditions for market-led economic growth and private sector development.

The institutions of contemporary planning practice

The final section of this chapter looks at the current planning system and highlights how it is embedding growth dependence and failing to offer institutional arrangements for an alternative. It covers the period from the replacement of the New Labour government by a Conservative-Liberal Democrat Coalition in 2010. The institutional areas covered are central governmental policy guidance, local plan making, planning regulation and community engagement.

Central government policy

Central government policy has considerable importance within the UK planning system (and while the discussion here is primarily about the situation in England, the influence of the devolved governments' policy frameworks is just as significant). As will be outlined below, this policy influences plan making at the local level and regulatory decisions, both those undertaken at this local level and those that pass to central government. Therefore, the current government's take on growth and the planning system as expressed in central policy guidance is highly significant.

Until 2012 central government guidance was captured in a number of Planning Policy Statements together with minerals policy guidance, circulars to local authorities and letters to Chief Planning Offices. The sheer volume of this guidance meant that there was always a opportunity to pick and choose which particular document and which specific section within that document would be most influential. In 2012 central government issued the National Planning Policy Framework (NPPF) setting out the essential elements of central government guidance for spatial planning at local government level in England; this mirrors similar documents for Scotland, Wales and Northern Ireland.[13] This was a bold step providing a single unified statement of central government policy. While some areas – notably policy in travelling communities and waste planning – remain outside the remit of the NPPF, this 60-page document does represent a relatively concise statement of central government's approach to planning. In relation to major infrastructure projects – such as energy pipelines or transmission cables, wind turbines, roads or power stations – there is additional central government policy guidance in the form of National Policy Statements (NPSs), which are debated and approved by the Houses of Parliament and set in the context of a National Infrastructure Plan.[14]

The current framing of central government guidance in the NPPF and NPSs is very similar; all commentators are clear on the strong growth orientation within these documents. In the NPSs, the majority of the documentation concerns details of the proposed development, outlining what would and would not constitute an acceptable proposal. But this is in the context of an overwhelming emphasis across these NPSs on the importance of allowing such infrastructure to go ahead in order to support economic growth. There is a similar message within the NPPF. The first chapter is entitled 'Building a strong, competitive economy' and the Ministerial foreword makes it clear that the purpose of planning is to help achieve sustainable development and that:

> *Development* means growth. We must accommodate the new ways by which we will earn our living in a competitive world.... Our lives, and the places in which we live them, can be better, but they will certainly be worse if things stagnate. (p i, original emphasis)

The framing is within the broader agenda of sustainable development, an acknowledgement of the influence of more than 25 years of campaigning for global environmental issues to be taken more seriously. However, it should be noted that in the Ministerial foreword it is stated that 'Sustainable development is about change', 'about positive growth' and the planning system 'is about helping to make this happen.' Thus the first statement under the heading 'Delivering sustainable development' (p 6) is: 'The Government is committed to securing economic growth in order to create jobs and prosperity.' Furthermore, the NPPF continues, 'The Government is committed to ensuring that the planning system does everything it can to support sustainable economic growth. Planning should operate to encourage and not act as an impediment to sustainable growth. Therefore significant weight should be placed on the need to support economic growth through the planning system.' And just to make it even clearer, the NPPF then states: 'To help achieve economic growth, local planning authorities should plan proactively to meet the development needs of business and support an economy fit for the 21st century.'

The NPPF formally reintroduces the presumption in favour of development that existed under the 1980s Conservative government, albeit in a slightly different form: 'Development that is sustainable should go ahead, without delay – a presumption in favour of sustainable development that is the basis for every plan, and every decision.' Planning is therefore about facilitating development and this development, while described as needing to be sustainable, is clearly assumed to be market-led. In Section 7 it is emphasised that the planning system will contribute to 'building a strong, responsive and competitive economy by ensuring that sufficient land of the right type is available in the right places and at the right time to support growth and innovation' and further 'by identifying and coordinating development requirements, including the provision of infrastructure' (p 2). This will be achieved by better understanding of the 'requirements' of market actors: 'Every effort should be made objectively to identify and then meet the housing, business and other development needs of an area, and respond positively to wider opportunities for growth. Plans should take account of market signals' (p 5). Thus the NPPF states that 'Local planning authorities should have a clear understanding of business needs within the economic markets operating in and across their areas' (p 39).

One area where this is particularly apparent is in terms of releasing land for housing development where it is clearly stated that the planning system should 'boost significantly the supply of housing' and do so by identifying five years' supply of 'specific deliverable sites' measured against locally identified market and affordable housing needs, but also providing an additional 5 per cent 'buffer', rising to a 20 per cent buffer in areas where 'there has been a record of persistent under delivery of housing' (p 12). This builds on an element of the planning system that has been apparent since 1980 – the involvement of housebuilders working with planners to identify sites for market-led development of housing.[15]

As Chapter 3 explores in more detail, growth-dependent planning argues that social and environmental benefits can be negotiated with developers once profitable market-led development has been permitted. However, the NPPF makes it clear that such negotiation should not threaten the viability of the development itself: 'To ensure viability, the costs of any requirements likely to be applied to development ... should, when taking account of the normal cost of development and mitigation, provide competitive returns to a willing land owner and willing developer to enable the development to be deliverable' (p 41). The link between deliverability within the planning system and market viability based on growth is thus clearly stated. Indeed this has been expanded into a requirement for local authorities to assess the impact of their plans as a whole on the viability of development in the area.[16]

The NPPF is a clear expression of the logic of growth-dependent planning. It is also at the end of a spectrum of interpretation closer to the deregulatory approach than was prevalent during the New Labour years. Much commentary has focused on this shift, but the relevant point is its continued espousal of growth-dependent *planning*. As such, the NPPF is intended to impose this form of growth-dependent planning on plan making and regulatory decision making throughout the planning system, and it leaves little scope for any alternative approach to be adopted.

Local plan making

There are two main reasons why local plan making will be strongly influenced by the paradigm of growth dependence. The first relates to the importance of central government policy guidance, currently the NPPF. The second concerns the indicative nature of UK planning and the relationship between local plans and development opportunities.

The NPPF is so influential within local planning because it is a core principle of the UK planning system that planning at the local level has to have regard to central government policy guidance. This is expressed in terms of the need for conformity between planning documents at different scales with central government policy carrying more weight in cases of conflict. Thus neighbourhood plans, prepared by neighbourhood forums under the 2011 Localism Act, have to be in conformity with local plans prepared by local planning authorities, and these have to be in conformity with central government planning guidance, including centrally the NPPF. Central government guidance, therefore, influences the substantive content of local plans being prepared at local authority and neighbourhood scales. Insofar as the NPPF represents the ideology of growth-dependent planning, so too will these local planning documents. Where a lower-level plan does not follow the policy guidance of a higher-tier plan or policy statement, then the lower-level plan carries less force and, in this way, policy influence cascades down from the NPPF.

For example, it has been shown that parish plans prepared by parish councils have tended to be ignored within the planning system because they did not integrate well into the local development plan prepared by the local authority. The language, structure and concerns were frequently too far apart to enable the parish plan to be an influence on the Local Development Framework (the form of the local plan at the time of this research). The same researchers, Gallent and Robinson, concluded that because neighbourhood planning exists within the context of an overriding commitment to permitting (sustainable) development to go ahead, as set out in the NPPF and also within the local plans that are charged with implementing the national strategy at local authority level, neighbourhood plans will not be able to reject developments and will instead be focused on more specific aspects of amending development options decided at local plan level. As the final sentence of their book states: 'Community input, even in a world of inflated rhetoric, will remain secondary to strategic necessity in the face of growth' (p 177).[17]

The second reason for local planning to be growth dependent relates to the nature of plans as indicative planning tools. It is possible to draw up a plan for an area with the intention of delivering significant social and environmental benefits – say, concentrated urban development focused on the town centre, a greener public realm, affordable housing provision, new public transport infrastructure, and so on – but the problem is whether the dynamics of a market-led process will drive development activity that complies with this plan. Under indicative planning, the plan is supposed to guide development decisions but, under a market-led system, it is the development sector that has control over where and when it will propose that development should occur. In terms of the location of development, there is a struggle here between planners indicating that they wish new development to follow a certain spatial pattern – because that will deliver benefits to the community – and developers who are looking to buy land cheaply and make a profit by building it out with higher value development. Land purchases may not fit with the planners' desired development pattern and so projects may come forward seeking planning permission that fall outside the intended land allocations in the plan.

The hope of indicative planning is that the publication of the plan and indeed the involvement of all key stakeholders – including developers – in drawing up the plan will act as a guide to the land-purchasing activities of developers. But in practice planners may be faced with a decision as to whether to refuse planning permission and forego the immediate prospect of urban development with all its attendant benefits and potential for planning gain in the hope of forcing this or another developer to come forward with a site that does conform to the plan. It is also notable that planning gain may be more readily negotiated on sites that have been bought cheaply (and thus have more development profit to share), and these sites are more likely to be those *not* identified in the plan (these dynamics are discussed further in Chapters 3 and 8). Thus there may be a tension between firm local plan land allocations and the ability to reap benefits through planning gain on more profitable developments.

However, there is also the possibility of the reverse happening. Indeed, in the UK, where land availability exercises involve planners and developers in discussions with each other over which sites are most likely to be developed, and these exercises feed directly into the local planning process,[18] it can regularly be the case that developer-identified land allocations strongly influence the drawing up of spatial frameworks. Here, if land that developers have already purchased (without the certainty of planning permission and hence at lower prices) is allocated for development, not only is there more certainty of the development going ahead, but there may be more scope for planning gain from a share of the enhanced development profits. Under such arrangements, growth dependence is even more firmly embedded as the market is leading the land allocation process within the plan itself.

In planning systems that seek to take a stronger line on where development should occur, the tools of public landownership or public sector investment in infrastructure are typically used to direct development to desirable locations. Indicative planning on its own remains a relatively weak planning tool and this reinforces the ideology of growth dependence as expressed in central government policy guidance and in local and even neighbourhood plans.

It should be noted that the Coalition government is also reviving policy initiatives from the 1980s that effectively remove certain delimited areas from the remit of local planning. The 2011 Budget announced a new wave of Enterprise Zones where, as well as certain taxation reliefs, 'radically simplified planning approaches' can apply, such as using Local Development Orders that permit development to go ahead without the need for specific planning permission (see also below).[19]

Planning regulation

The importance of central government policy carries through into regulatory decision making on planning applications for permission to develop largely because of the role of the planning appeal system. This is the system whereby planning applicants who have been refused planning permission by a local authority can appeal to central government in the form of the Planning Inspectorate.[20] A planning inspector will re-examine the case and has the power to uphold the refusal of planning permission or to grant that permission directly. So if a developer finds their ability to obtain planning permission on a specific project is being constrained because the local authority is not taking full account of central government policy, then they can appeal to the Inspectorate on those grounds. If the inspector agrees, then they are very likely – *ceteris paribus* – to override the local decision. This will have the effect of guiding local planning regulation more firmly towards taking account of central government policy as local authorities do not wish to expend resources – including possibly the other party's costs – on contesting planning appeals which they then lose. If central government guidance expresses the importance of a growth-dependent approach, this will, therefore, be given expression and effect through planning regulation decisions.

However, planning regulation also has to follow a range of other requirements arising from the statutory basis of the planning system, the operation of the appeals system and the occasional intervention of the law courts into planning matters. For example, planning regulation has to have regard to the relevant development plans and also 'other material considerations', although the contents of the development plan are intended to prevail unless there is a good argument to the contrary.[21] These 'other material considerations' are often site-related and/or concern details of the planning application. And there are constraints on what can count as a 'material consideration' so that matters considered not relevant to land use may be excluded. Precedent (the kinds of decisions that have been made in the past) also plays a role, either directly in terms of making links between current and past decisions, or indirectly in terms of the fear of creating a new precedent.

And so on.... Some of these more detailed aspects of how planning regulation currently works will be discussed in Chapters 7–9, particularly Chapter 8. As will be seen, the current operation of planning regulation constrains the possibilities for pursuing more innovative and non–growth-dependent modes of planning. Chapter 10 comes back to these details in discussing proposals for reforming the operation of planning regulation in the future.

Planning regulation also has to have some regard to the extent to which a local community is in favour of a development proposal, although that is never the main basis of decision making, given the importance of the development plan and established forms of 'other material considerations'. That said, there will be scope for pressure from community and other groups, as the next section explores. Some groups will seek to resist the development, some to support it and some to try and reshape it through negotiations within the regulatory process. The existence of regulatory control by planning authorities over development proposals is, however, important in structuring relationships between the local community and the planning authority since the attitudes of community groups may be significantly influenced by the extent of beneficial planning gain that they believe can be achieved by negotiation during regulatory decision making. More prospect of planning gain may, quite reasonably, reduce the scale of objections to a development.

However, it has been emphasised that the potential for planning gain, while reliant on the existence of this regulation and the power this gives local planners when negotiating with developers, is limited by the financial realities of urban development. So there is a strong incentive for communities to support development which is highly profitable in market terms if they believe that it can also deliver community benefits. One reform that has recently been put into legislative form is that developers will be able to return to a negotiated agreement on planning gain and argue that economic conditions have altered so that the agreed level of community benefit (specifically affordable housing) can no longer be delivered. This reform, included in the 2013 Growth and Infrastructure Act, is both a clear statement of growth dependence and also a restructuring of planning regulation that undermines the ability of local authorities to be clear on the community benefits they are negotiating and of local communities to judge the relative benefits of a development proposal.

It should be noted that there have been some tendencies to take more areas of development out of planning control altogether in line with the revived use of Enterprise Zones. The Use Classes Order (which sets out the need – or not – for planning permission when changing the use of a building) has been altered, ostensibly to fit better with the emerging demands of businesses, and the General Permitted Development Order (which permits certain small-scale developments to take place without the need for specific planning permission) has also been amended to allow more householder developments, including installation of micro-renewable energy equipment, to go ahead. A significant alteration to the Use Classes Order that is currently in process concerns the ability to convert offices to residential use without the need for planning permission, although local authorities can apply for a local exemption to this relaxation of planning regulation. This and other changes to planning regulation are discussion further in Chapter 8.

Finally there are some areas – outside the appeals system – where central government takes the regulatory decision on development directly. To date this applies mainly to major infrastructure projects. Under the 2008 Planning Act, proposals for nationally significant infrastructure projects are subject to a distinct planning regime, in which the proposal is considered by an examining inspector from the National Infrastructure Directorate of the Planning Inspectorate.[22] The decision – which is formally taken by the Secretary of State following a report by the inspector – must be based on the guidance provided in the NPSs issued by central government. As discussed above, the current batch of NPSs set out a range of criteria that may be considered in making this decision, but they also identify a range of factors that cannot be considered relevant. However, the main thrust of the NPSs is supportive of the need for infrastructure investment and thus likely to be strongly in favour of proposals that come forward. Central government has extended this system for regulating infrastructure projects to other major commercial projects under the Growth and Infrastructure Act, which is likely to increase their likelihood of gaining planning consent, perhaps at the expense of planning gain that could have been negotiated at the local level.

Community engagement

The above discussion suggests that there is strong evidence that a weakly regulated form of growth-dependent planning is currently embedded in the institutions of the planning system. This arises from the content of central government guidance; the principle of conformity of plans with higher-tier plans and ultimately central government guidance; the arguments for allocating sites for development which are put forward by developers in order to capitalise on development opportunities and to maximise the potential for planning gain from development; the need to have regard to central government guidance in planning regulation; the pressures for local communities to grant planning permission in anticipation of achieving planning gain and other side-benefits; and current tendencies towards relaxing specific aspects of planning regulation.

However, community engagement also remains a key element of the planning system. For all its espousal of a growth-dependent agenda, this is recognised within the NPPF. There are references to 'empowering local people to shape their surroundings' and planning being 'a creative exercise in finding ways to enhance and improve the places in which people live their lives' (p 5). When it comes to discussing 'Promoting healthy communities' (p 17), it begins by emphasising that 'Local authorities should create a shared vision with communities of the residential environment and facilities they wish to see' and that the aim should be 'to involve all sections of the community in the development of Local Plans and in planning decisions', and further to ensure engagement is 'early and meaningful' (p 37). The promotion of neighbourhood planning through the 2011 Localism Act provides new opportunities for community participation and the NPPF seeks to support this. It describes neighbourhood plans as giving 'communities direct power to develop a shared vision for their neighbourhood and deliver the sustainable development they need' (p 37). As well as potentially drawing up the neighbourhood plan, local residents can vote in a referendum on adopting the plan.

How does this mesh with the already identified tendencies towards growth dependence in the system? The above discussion has highlighted how there are incentives for local communities to welcome market-led development for the planning gain it offers. The problem is that such planning gain may not always meet the needs of all communities within a locality or sufficiently offset undesirable features of the market-led development itself, as perceived by those communities. It is important that all communities within an area are able to express an opinion on this. But in practice, community and broader stakeholder engagement is shaped by the institutions put in place for such engagement and the way that people come forward to participate.

Following the logic of governance and collaborative planning approaches, local planning is based on the engagement of a range of stakeholders including the public and specific local communities; this is firmly embedded within the statutory framework and established planning practice. Indeed under the planning system instituted by the 2004 Planning and Compulsory Purchase Act a key document that had to be produced by the local authority was the Statement of Community Involvement. This detailed the ways in which the authority intended to engage local residents and other key people and organisations during the preparation of plans.

In relation to local plans, the body charged with engaging organisations across the local authority area is the Local Strategic Partnership under the 2000 Local Government Act but, under Coalition government reforms, Local Enterprise Partnerships have emerged as important forums, replacing Regional Development Agencies. These (unelected) bodies usually have community representatives on it but, as Gallent and Robinson have identified, representing the local community viewpoint in general is not the same as representing the needs and views and values of specific local communities and groups.[23] How these people represent their local community will depend on them as individuals as well as the diversity of that community.

Furthermore, different communities within a locality have different resources and powers. The potential of network power relies on the recognition of interdependencies, as Innes and Booher make clear (see Chapter 1). But local, particularly lower-income, communities may not be able to demonstrate important interdependencies that give them access to network power within planning deliberations.[24] In addition the collective action problem often disadvantages certain local communities. This refers to the structural disincentive to engage with a planning issue where the perceived costs of being involved (which are certain, happening now and falling on a specific group, that is, those who choose to be involved) outweigh the apparent benefits of influencing planning policy and decision making (benefits that are uncertain, occurring in the future and likely to benefit the wider local community). The collective action problem highlights that it is in the interests of most people to free-ride on others' involvement and willingness to prepare a plan rather than get involved themselves.[24] Therefore it tends to be a rather specific group of people who take the lead in planning, a group that is not necessarily representative of all residents or the most vulnerable among those residents. Research has emphasised that much community-level planning is led by a vocal and active minority.[26]

It is a perennial problem within planning systems that higher-income communities have been both more able to mobilise opposition within the windows offered by the planning system and to be effective in affecting the actual decisions taken. This is due to a number of factors, including: the other pressures on lower income households that prevent them having the time to participate; the greater resources that higher-income households are able to bring to mobilisation efforts; the knowledge of the planning process itself that higher-income households can muster so that they are able to mobilise in a way that is more likely to be effective; perhaps even some degree of prejudice or lack of care for lower-income communities among planning decision makers; or, to put it another way, considerable concern among local politicians for the political power that higher-income households may be able to exercise.

The situation with regard to future major infrastructure projects is even less attentive to local people's needs. The system for approving major infrastructure projects, introduced in the 2008 Planning Act, has been widely criticised for the way in which it has constrained the opportunities for participation.[27] Here the inspector oversees a process in which written material is produced and exchanged between parties and, then, a public examination is held at which only those authorised by the inspector are allowed to attend. This replaced the former Public Local Inquiry systems in which everyone had a right to attend and speak, although their evidence was given less weight if they did not open themselves to cross-examination. But, in addition to these procedural changes, it is clear that the decision-making process itself gives less weight to the views of local communities, even if they are allowed to attend and speak at the examination, since the NPSs are the main reference point in justifying any decision.

This will have greater significance in the future, given current government changes to extend the remit of the National Infrastructure Directorate within the Planning Inspectorate to major commercial developments, as mentioned above. This would remove such development proposals from any remaining influence of local communities and tie in the decisions on such developments even more closely to the weakly regulated growth-dependent planning paradigm set out in the NPPF.

This review, therefore, demonstrates across the areas of central government policy, plan making, regulation and community engagement, first, that growth-dependent planning is the dominant paradigm in British planning and, second, that the current trend is towards a less tightly regulated version of this paradigm.

THREE

The growth-dependent planning paradigm

T he aim of this book is to challenge the dominance of the paradigm of growth-dependent planning and suggest, not necessarily a replacement, but an alternative approach that may be more appropriate in certain localities and at certain times. But before this alternative is mapped out, we need to understand the current paradigm and its limitations more fully. This chapter explores the paradigm of growth-dependent planning. The subsequent two chapters then derive a critique looking, first, in Chapter 4 at the important underlying economic assumptions of the paradigm and, then, in Chapter 5 at the social and environmental consequences of relying on growth dependence.

The argument for growth-dependent planning comprises two elements. First, there is the assumption that attracting investment in new development is, in itself, of benefit to the locality and the local community. Second, there is the emphasis on the potential for the development to generate funding for other side-benefits for the community, commonly known as planning gain. This chapter develops these arguments, but first it provides a summary account of the economic model of urban development underpinning the paradigm.

The economic model underpinning growth-dependent planning

Behind the paradigm of growth-dependent planning lies a particular view of urban change rooted in neo-classical economics.[1] Here urban change is a response to the prices set by land and property markets and, in particular, developers respond to the gap between the price of a site in its existing use and the potential price if developed for a new use.

This can be illustrated most readily by considering the pressures for greenfield development. Agricultural land prices in June 2010 were in the order of £15,400 per hectare for England; the price of residential development land for July 2010 was £1.75 million for England excluding London.[2] This price for housebuilding land is largely determined by the price of new housing, itself influenced by a variety of factors including demographic change, wage levels and the availability of mortgage lending. Even allowing for the different location of agricultural and development land, the gap between agricultural and residential development land prices is considerably larger than the costs of turning farmland into a housing estate, and thus acts as a continuous pressure for agricultural land to be developed for housing. This pressure is often resisted. For example, landowners may refuse to sell to residential development as with farmers who wish to remain in farming or agricultural investors who wish to retain a long-term interest in the capital appreciation of agricultural land. Furthermore, planning regulation, with the support of local communities and environmental non-governmental organisations (NGOs), may control the location of residential development, seeking to steer it away from such greenfield sites.

A similar principle also underpins development decisions in other locations. An inner-city site of small light industrial units could be a profitable development opportunity for offices if the value of the site for industry is below that for commercial use. This is often expressed in terms of the demand for industrial units being low and that for offices being high. What is meant here is that organisations are willing to pay more for offices on the site than industrial users would be. It does not mean that there are necessarily more bidders for offices than for industrial units – demand is not higher for offices than industrial units in quantitative terms of the number of potential buyers or renters. Rather, demand is higher for one use than the other in terms of willingness and ability to pay, in monetary terms.

This discrepancy in the demand for industrial units and offices will be given expression in terms of industrial and commercial rents and capital values for industrial and office buildings. This then translates into prices for land in these different uses. Once the price differential between the value of the offices and the price of the industrial site exceeds the costs of clearance and development of the new offices, market signals are favouring redevelopment and urban change.

Figure 3.1 illustrates this. It shows how a changing market value for a completed development on a site affects the viability of that development project. At Point A, the market value does not even cover the development and land costs; there is no scope for the developer to make a profit at this price for the completed development. The only way that a profit could be engineered is by negotiating the land costs down with the landowner, if that is possible. But at Point A, even if land costs were driven down to zero, it looks as if the market value of the development would only just cover development costs, again leaving little if any profit for the developer.

By Point B, a break-even point has been reached where the development value (usually termed Gross Development Value) covers all the costs of developing and the land costs (land price plus all finance and fees involved in purchasing and holding the site). However, there is still no developer profit at this point. Only if the development value increases further, moving towards Point C, does the developer begin to get a return on the work involved in progressing the development and the risk that has been borne.

Figure 3.1: Development viability

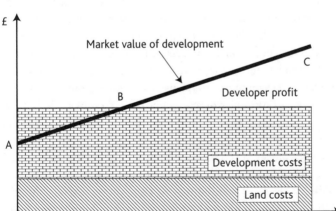

Whether this is enough return to get the developer to put the project into action depends on how the profitability of this project compares to that for other projects that the developer could be undertaking or to other investments that the developer could put their money into or raise funding for.

In any market, there is usually a 'rule of thumb' for what constitutes an acceptable developer's profit, say 25 per cent of all development costs or 12.5 per cent of the Gross Development Value. This 'rule of thumb' becomes embedded in property markets through the accepted practices of valuation. The main way of valuing development land is called the 'residual method' and it operates on a fairly simple formula that encapsulates the logic of the economic model described above:[3]

	Gross Development Value
Less	Total Development Costs
Equals	Residual Value available for purchase of development site

In this formulation (which is slightly different from that represented in Figure 3.1), Total Development Costs include an element for the minimum profit a developer would need to make to attract them to this opportunity calculated using the 'rule of thumb' that the valuation profession agrees is appropriate.

However, there may also be specific circumstances associated with any particular development project that could affect the level of profit that the developer considers acceptable. Perhaps the developer has become so committed to this scheme that a lower profit level will be accepted provided that the site can be built out and the development sold on. Any profit might be acceptable provided an exit strategy can be implemented. Or there may be corporate circumstances within the development company that make it more important to complete this particular development project even at a lower than usually acceptable profit level. Perhaps this development represents a new marketing strategy for an emerging niche, such as housing for young singles or retired couples or for the energy-conscious. It may also be the case that completing this development is essential for building a closer relationship with a local authority and thus open up the possibility of greater ease in getting planning permissions for other sites, perhaps purchased on more favourable terms from the developer's point of view.

In general, however, the logic of this approach is that the low value of land is considered a signal for potential redevelopment, and that higher value land uses will be the desired outcome of urban change. The linguistic slippage between prices and values is significant here; higher priced land and developments are viewed as more valuable, more valued by society. A row of shops let out at low rents with relatively cheap flats above is, in this perspective, worth less to society than the row of new terraced housing that could replace it, aimed at higher-income consumers in the residential market. The brownfield site that is largely vacant – and therefore has no current use value in market terms – is worth less than the retail warehouse estate that could replace it. And so on....

The core dynamic here is that market processes generate new development by being oriented to making profit from those with purchasing power. This does not mean that all development has to be aimed at the highest value end of the market, those with the most purchasing power. Much depends on the balance between the demand for new property in the market and all the costs of providing that development, including materials, professional fees and labour and also land and finance. This can mean that the gap between development prices and costs of provision is such that market actors consider medium rather than high priced to be the appropriate niche to try and fill in a specific location at a particular time.

However, it does mean that there are likely to be difficulties in providing new market development aimed at those with the least purchasing power whether in the residential, commercial or industrial sectors. This will only occur if land is provided very cheaply for some reason or if the costs of construction can be kept low or Gross Development Value can be increased by building at higher densities. As a result development aimed at lower-income households and small companies (the 'S' of SMEs, small and medium-sized enterprises) are often of poorer construction standards, densely developed and built on sites that are considered, for various reasons, as less attractive locations. And if circumstances change so that higher-value development can be built at a greater profit on the site, then the competitive forces within the market will favour the higher-value over the lower-value end use.

The arguments for developing a planning paradigm on this model of market-led development are based on the perceived benefits of promoting such development. The next two sections set out these arguments.

The direct and consequential benefits of promoting development

So growth-dependent planning works by responding to market signals for determining where and when development should occur. Site allocation policies in plans may seek to steer that development into certain sites, urban zones and regions but, within this paradigm, planners have to work with market processes and often find they have to facilitate and promote market-led development. An essential element of this is identifying and encouraging higher-priced land uses to replace lower-priced ones as a means of promoting urban change. Why should this be seen as a desirable task for planners?

First, it is assumed that higher land values reflect higher development values and that these, in turn, are related to more demand for the activities that will take place within those developments and buildings. Such activities fulfil important economic and social functions. Therefore promoting high-value development is a way of recognising there is unfulfilled demand for much-needed activities. Put another way, people and companies want to use the higher-value developments so much that they are willing to pay more for them and this prompts urban development to occur. Thus growth-dependent planning ensures currently unfulfilled demand is met through urban change.

A good example of this is provided by brownfield development.[4] In the UK this term is used to refer to development on land that has been previously developed but is now vacant; brownfield land is not necessarily contaminated, as is the case in the USA. According to growth-dependent planning, putting any new economically viable use on the land will be beneficial, replacing land with no use and hence no market value with both a positive use and a positive value.

Indeed, even if the site is not completely vacant, redeveloping a lower-value site – say, an industrial site – with a higher-value use – say, commercial offices – will still be considered advantageous as the new use is meeting a higher-value demand of greater worth to society.

What is important here is the value as determined by market transactions between buyers or renters with money and those land or property owners who would like to receive money. Any other ways in which the site is valued by people and groups in society is not captured in this notion of 'value'. Environmental economists have argued in particular that ecosystem services and assets are often undervalued or ignored by such market transactions because they are effectively being offered as a public good or free gift to society.[5] Thus the apparently 'empty' brownfield site, which could be a profitable development site, may currently be a habitat for a variety of animal and flora species or be in a riverine floodplain or absorb urban run-off in sudden downpours or fulfil a role in managing the local climate or improve local air quality or.... None of these benefits of the site in its current undeveloped state would influence its market value which, if it is unused, is probably extremely low.

Environmental economists have devised a variety of techniques to try and put a monetary value on such ecosystem services, using proxy market prices or statistical analysis or survey-based techniques to come up with an appropriate figure.[6] These figures may play a role in government decisions about policy, regulation or subsidies, but the key point remains that these figures will not be taken into account by individual markets actors – the developers and landowners – and thus they have little relevance to the argument for the fundamental benefit to society of market-led development meeting demand as expressed within property and land markets.

Second, development itself is a form of economic activity that creates both wealth – in the form of new capital assets of buildings and developments – and income – in the form of profits for developers, land sales for landowners, wages and fees for people working on the projects and contracts for all manner of suppliers of materials and services. Such wealth and income creation is the motor of a capitalist economy and thus growth-dependent planning contributes to national economic well-being as well as meeting localised demand through promoting new development. The employment and wealth-creation potential of the development industry is often particularly valued in economic downturns when it can be seen as a means of engineering a recovery. Even in the low growth context of 2010 (Q4 or fourth quarter) the construction industry accounted for employment of 2.23 million people and contributed £18.9 million to national output from new work, with an additional £11 million from repair and maintenance.[7]

This employment and wealth creation is not just limited to the construction activities themselves but also linked to the jobs associated with the new pattern of urban land uses and the new buildings and their occupants. And it is a key theorem within economics that economic activity can generate more economic activity in a virtuous cycle.[8] Thus the higher-value economic activities occupying the new developments will have a multiplier effect. For example, if a new shopping centre is built, people will spend more on buying goods and services there. This will result in revenue for the retail companies and wages for those who work there. The wages will support more local spending and some of the retail revenue may be ploughed back into the local economy, through paying for goods and services to local firms (although it may well flow through to companies and people outside the locality – see Chapter 5).

This multiplier effect will also have a spatial dimension. Where one area has been redeveloped for a higher-value use, then there is the potential for spatial spillover effects. This occurs when the new development enhances the use of nearby sites, increasing the demand for them and making them more valuable. Replacing a run-down row of garages with new housing may, if well designed, make the surrounding housing more valuable. A new commercial development may pull up the rents and prices of nearby existing offices and shops if the entire area is now deemed more attractive. This can lead to development activity spreading outwards as the potential value of new buildings grows, bringing unused sites into active occupation and replacing old with new property stock.

These consequential benefits of urban development are argued to create trickle-down effects, whereby the benefits of local economic growth – stimulated by the physical urban development – spread within the local community to create benefits that also eventually accrue to lower-income households.[9] Owners of lower-priced properties will see the value of those properties rise, but as the lowest-income households are less likely to be owner-occupiers, they will not see much benefit. Furthermore, these trickle-down benefits are largely going to arise from employment creation in the locality associated with inward movement of the more profitable businesses that are able to pay the increased rents and property prices.

This is the logic behind the redevelopment of the Elephant and Castle area in South London (but this case could describe many, many other locations across the country).[10] This area, while a vibrant local economy and entertainment centre at the turn of the last century, has been characterised for the last half-century by its existence as a major road and public transport interchange with a mix of modernist council housing, office blocks and an infamous shopping centre, opened in 1965 reputedly as the first covered shopping mall in Europe. However, the area has, for this period, fallen outside the remit of the central London property market, with high levels of social deprivation; the shopping centre quickly became a 'white elephant' and even painting it bright pink and putting a statue of an elephant on top for a time did little to reduce vacancies and raise rents.

The increase in property values along the south bank of the Thames – starting to the west near Waterloo and Westminster and then spreading east towards Tower Bridge, passing the new Tate Modern gallery, the replica Shakespeare Globe theatre and then Hay's Galleria and into More London and City Hall – suggested to the London Borough of Southwark that redevelopment of the Elephant and Castle area could bring the locality within the influence of this central London property market and start a chain reaction of increasing property values. To this end the current plan for the area amounts to a £1.5 billion scheme for 55 acres, including a new pedestrianised shopping centre, a market square, up to 450,000 square feet of retail space and 5,000 new and replacement homes. This, in the council's words, 'will create a new exciting destination for London'.[11]

The side-benefits of promoting development

In addition to these assumed direct and consequential benefits of growth-dependent planning, scope also exists for using the regulatory powers of the planning system to direct some of the profits of new urban development to meet the needs of local communities. Thus an additional argument for growth-dependent planning is that it enables the funding of specific benefits to the broader local community. Here there is an important role for planners within growth-dependent planning based on their negotiation skills and also fundamentally on the control that they exercise through planning regulation. The term 'planning gain' is generally used to describe the channelling of a share of development profits to such community benefits. Thus the Elephant and Castle redevelopment outlined above is proposed to include new leisure and cultural facilities, improvements to the public realm including new open spaces and landscaping, and also access to local employment and training opportunities.

A variety of mechanisms have been used over time to enable planning gain to be successfully achieved. In many cases the exact nature and extent of the planning gain depends on negotiations between the planning authority (usually the case officer handling the planning application) and the developer. The planning officer has the benefit of his or her authority's regulatory powers since without the approval of the planning application, development cannot proceed. To this some officers add considerable negotiation skills, although perhaps these are not emphasised sufficiently in formal planning education, tending instead to be learned 'on the job'.[12] The developer, for their part, has knowledge of how far to go, in financial terms, in conceding commitments to community benefits. There will a point beyond which the viability of the development is undermined by the extent of planning gain agreed.

This is illustrated in Figure 3.2. This is similar to Figure 3.1 but it starts with a position on the vertical axis where there is sufficient developer's profit to make this a viable project. The diagram shows a new triangle for an increasing amount of planning gain that the planning authority has been able to negotiate. It is assumed that the planning gain not only benefits the wider community but also makes

Figure 3.2: Planning gain and development viability

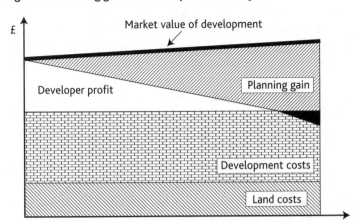

the development itself more attractive, as would be the case, say, with negotiating more green space. Thus the line for the market value of the development increases slightly as the amount of planning gain goes up. It is possible, though, to conduct the following argument assuming an unchanging development value or even one that falls with the amount of planning gain negotiated.

However, it is apparent that, even with the assumption of increasing development value, there comes a point where the increasing amount of planning gain starts to eat into the developer's profit to such an extent that it reduces that profit to zero and then starts to bite into the budget for development costs (the black triangle). At this point, it is clear that the extraction of planning gain is rendering the project unviable. Planners need to keep their negotiation of such planning gain to the left-hand side of the diagram if they wish the project to go ahead.

The ability of a planner to negotiate substantial planning gain depends on the context of regulatory control by the planning authority. This is the basis for the planner's power within the negotiations. Policies that weaken this regulatory control, for example, by establishing a firm presumption in favour of development, will reduce the amount of planning gain that can be achieved by local authorities. Support for the negotiation of planning gain in policies from local to central government level will increase the power of planning authorities. This will particularly be the case if central government (through the Planning Inspectorate) resists appeals against refusals of planning permission by local authorities unsatisfied with the willingness of developers to commit to requested planning gain.

Another factor will be the extent to which the planning officer has a good working knowledge of development appraisal; this will enhance their negotiation skills and ensure that they do not sell their community short. In some local authorities, a requirement to operate on an open book basis has been adopted. This requires trust between the planning authority and the developer, but enables community benefit to be openly negotiated rather than being a guessing game about the extent of the surplus profits available for planning gain. Otherwise developers are bound to argue that the viability of their project is being threatened by claims for planning gain well before the viability cut-off on Figure 3.2 is approached.

Once the level of planning gain has been negotiated, the agreement has to be established as a legal contract to be binding on the developer. This is currently done under a so-called Section 106 agreement (from the 1990 Town and Country Planning Act). These agreements are linked to the planning permission so that the permission is not valid unless the agreement is complied with. However, there is some doubt whether such agreements are actively enforced if the developer reneges on all or part of its content once the development is built out. Under measures within the 2013 Growth and Infrastructure Act, as mentioned above, these agreements may also be renegotiated if the developer can argue that economic circumstances have changed so that the project is no longer viable, that is, that the market value of the final development has fallen or shifted downwards in Figure 3.2 so that the quantum of planning gain (the shaded area) can no longer be sustained. In effect, the break-even point for the development has moved to the left in Figure 3.2.

Some councils have opted for a tariff approach to extracting planning gain rather than negotiating each planning application from scratch. Here there is a pre-set list of benefits that are expected from a development, with the scale of benefits linked directly to the scale of the development. The legal rationale here is that the developer is paying for the additional costs to the local authority of the development, including the need to provide additional school places, primary medical services, and so on. It is also argued that this gives the developer greater certainty in devising a scheme and thus assists their viability calculations.

For example, the London Borough of Southwark has a dedicated Section 106 website with an online interactive tool that enables the developer to enter the details of the proposed development and get an indication of the expected planning gain contributions (see Figure 3.3). To assist the process, the website also provides a template for a model legal agreement and, for the specific case of car-free developments, a model Section 106 Unilateral Undertaking that a developer can use to propose a planning gain package that will be acceptable to the council.

While such a tariff may seem more rigid than open negotiation on planning gain, in practice there will always be an element of negotiation in coming to the final agreement on each case. In the London Borough of Southwark, such negotiation has been used to get developers to contribute financial support for a project from their Community Project banks, which are collections of small-scale projects that have been proposed by local people. However, the developer may also use an open book approach to justify less planning gain being agreed than under the strict tariff approach on the basis that the profits from this particular development will not support the full tariff burden.

This ad hoc use of planning gain tariffs is now being affected by the roll-out of the Community Infrastructure Levy (CIL), introduced in the 2008 Planning Act.[13] Here the local planning authority devises a tariff on the basis of the infrastructure needs associated with the global scale of new development to be permitted in the locality. These infrastructure needs can cover road schemes, flood defences, schools, hospitals, other health and social care facilities, park improvements, green spaces and leisure centres. The total cost of this infrastructure is then divided by the quantum of expected development (that is, the global scale used to calculate the infrastructure needs) to produce a CIL per unit of development (per dwelling unit or per square metre). This approach builds on the innovative first use in Milton Keynes

Figure 3.3: London Borough of Southwark's Section 106 toolkit

Southwark Council

VERSION 2.14
Section 106 Planning Obligations Workbook

This workbook provides a tool to calculate the planning contributions required for a proposed development. Each worksheet covers a separate topic area. You can access each worksheet by clicking on the tabs at the bottom of the page. You should input the proposal data in the yellow boxes on this page. When you fill in these boxes on this first page, the data will up-date automatically to the following worksheets. There are also yellow boxes on the Public Realm and Site specific Transport worksheets where you should enter additional data, or you have the option of the worksheet calculating an 'indicative average' cost for your scheme. The calculation of the contributions is carried out automatically and a summary produced on the last worksheet, Planning Obligations Statement'.

YOU MUST FILL IN ALL THE YELLOW BOXES ON THE INTRODUCTION (THIS) WORKSHEET, PUBLIC REALM, TRANSPORT SITE-SPECIFIC, AND PLANNING OBLIGATIONS STATEMENT WORKSHEETS. If you have any problems, questions or feedback please contact the section 106 implementation team on 020 7525 7309

Residential	Total	Owner occupied	Social for rent	Intermediate	Habitable rooms	Units with children
Studio units		0			0	0
1 bedroom units		0			0	0
2 bedroom units		0			0	0
3 bedroom units		0			0	0
4 or more bedroom units		0			0	0
Total		0	0	0	0	0
Total residential units		0				

Affordable Housing

% of affordable housing on site (if to be provided through in-lieu payment enter 0)   **35**

Office (B1 space)

Net gross internal floor space sq m

Public Realm

For pre-application discussions ONLY, would you like to use an average indicative cost for public realm? (YES or NO)   **YES**

Open Space

Is it in an Area of District Park Deficiency (YES or NO)   **YES**

Affordable Housing in-lieu payment

For exceptional cases only. Which value area does the site lie in – 1 (site-by-site), 2 (£100,000/room), 3 (£80,000/room). This is based on 35% housing provision. See also

Affordable Housing Grant

Does the development have a full or partial grant from the Housing Corporation? (YES or NO)   **NO**

Retail (A1, A2, A3, A4, A5 space)

Net gross internal floor space sq m

Transport

For pre-application discussions ONLY, would you like to use an average indicative cost for site specific calculation? (YES or NO)   **YES**

In the Archaeology Priority Zone?

If yes, size or site in sq m?

FOR LARGE SCHEMES - number of archaeological weeks if over 6 weeks

Hotel

Number of rooms (up to 3 star hotel)	
Number of rooms (4 star plus hotel)	55
Number of rooms (Apart-hotel)	

Mayoral Community Infrastructure Levy (CIL)

Indicative chargeable floorspace in sq m   **10256**

Student Housing

Number of student bedspaces (based on number of beds, not units or clusters)

Employment

Will the developer be providing a certified employment training scheme during construction? (YES or NO)   **NO**

Transport for London

Enter any amount requested by Transport for London   **0**

Community Facilities

Is there an identified lack of community facilities in the area? (YES or NO)   **YES**

Crossrail charge

Is the site in the London Bridge and Bankside opportunity area? (YES or NO)   **NO**

If the site is a hotel please state floorspace

Source: www.southwark.gov.uk/downloads/download/2523/section_106_toolkit

48

of a 'roof tax' where £18,000 per dwelling was charged on new residential development to fund infrastructure investment.

To explain how this will affect the London Borough of Southwark, discussed above, in London the Greater London Authority has instituted a mayoral CIL and the London Borough of Southwark is now putting in a place a borough-level CIL to replace their Section 106 tariff. This does not mean that Section 106 agreements will no longer be negotiated in the borough; they just have to cover issues and benefits not covered by either of the CIL schemes.

It can be seen from this discussion that there has been a move away from planning gain constituting a series of individually negotiated community benefits on each development towards using planning gain measures to get a financial share of the development profits, effectively acting as a development tax. One consequence of this new form of planning gain is that it creates a strong incentive for local authorities as planning authorities to favour and encourage profitable, market-led development in their areas. This becomes a way to provide an addition to severely constrained local budgets. This is where discussion of planning gain, consequent on the exercise of planning regulation, begins to merge with discussion of local government finance.

In the UK, local government is heavily dependent on grants from central government for its budget, such grants being calculated according to a complex formula meant to represent the need for spending on various local government services. This is supplemented with returns from council tax, a tax on the beneficial occupation of domestic property, which is based on the capital value of housing (but where the rate of the tax can be 'capped' by central government). There is also a tax on non-domestic property; until April 2013 the tax rate was set by central government, the tax receipts – which amounted to £21.5 billion in 2010/11 – were passed to central government and this was then redistributed back to local government as part of their grant. Finally, fees and income for services provided by local government contributes to their budgets. In 2010/11, local authorities in England spent £172.4 billion, of which £22.1 billion was raised by council tax, £28.6 billion from fees, rents and other income, leaving all the rest (bar £6.2 billion of 'financial movements') to be covered by various grants.[14]

This mix of grants and taxes in itself provided only a weak set of incentives for encouraging more development in an area. However, there are now a range of measures and proposals seeking to create a more direct financial link between urban development and monetary receipts to local government. For example, there is the use of Tax Increment Funding introduced in the 2012 Local Government Finance Act. Here investment in infrastructure in locality, usually transport infrastructure, is funded by a loan secured on the anticipated increased tax yield from property taxes resulting from the increase in property values that will be due to the infrastructure investment.

Generalising this approach, Manchester City Council has been able to negotiate a deal with central government in which they have been permitted to keep a share of the increased tax yield – not just property taxes but also income and corporation tax – that is expected to result from investment in the regeneration of the city. Some of the government's so-called City Deals also take this approach, although none is as extensive as the deal with Manchester City Council.[15] They can now also be seen in the context of the Single Local Growth Fund, under which central government funding will be devolved down to Local Enterprise Partnerships to manage on the basis of strategic multi-year plans for local growth, Local Growth Deals. This initiative arises from the Heseltine review that reported in 2012.[16]

This trend towards allowing a share of the increased tax yield – property, corporation and/or income taxes – to be kept by local government and then be available for local spending on community services and assets is a powerful way of embedding the arguments for growth-dependent planning within local government culture more generally. It suggests that the promotion of market-led development will generate financial benefits through increased tax yield which can then be available for local community needs in a much more generalised way than the negotiation of planning gain on specific developments.

The reforms to local government finance that came into effect in April 2013 are the biggest changes in this direction. The 2012 Local Government Finance Act allows local government to keep up to half the business rates generated in their area and further retain any new rates (from new 'hereditaments' or buildings) for a seven-year period. A system of 'tariffs' and 'top-ups' ensures that no local authority loses out when the reforms come into effect but clearly, thereafter, local authorities that encourage more development, particularly high-value development, will benefit financially. However, this is tempered by the application of a 'levy' to match the increase in business rates growth to the increase in local authority spending power (that is, clawing back some receipts from local authorities with an unusually high quantity of business properties in their area); this levy will be used as a safety net for local authorities whose income falls, for example, if a major local business closes. These reforms are explicitly designed to align local authority budgets more closely to local business growth.

And the already effective New Homes Bonus, introduced in April 2011, can also be seen in this light.[17] Here local communities – potentially at a scale below the local authority level – can benefit from additional finance proportionate to the amount of new market housebuilding that is permitted in their area. The finance would be equivalent to six years of the net additional council tax from new build, with affordable housing attracting an additional bonus. This finance is then available for local authorities to spend as they wish, although close consultation with communities affected by new development is expected. The aim is to potentially diffuse the tension between existing residents, on the one hand, and provision for incoming homebuyers and renters, on the other.

There is, therefore, a potent mix of arguments for the growth-dependent planning approach based on the value of the development that it promotes and permits, the additional benefits extracted in the form of additional tax revenue, money for infrastructure investment and specifically negotiated planning gain, as well as broader enhanced economic activity in the locality.

FOUR

The flawed economic assumptions of growth-dependent planning

The previous chapter set out the key assumptions and elements of the growth-dependent model of planning. This has made it clear that growth-dependent planning has two requirements if it is to be effective. First, it needs regulatory control to deliver social and environmental benefits from market-led development. Second, it assumes economic growth to drive such market-led development. Chapter 2 has already shown that ideological and political shifts often result in regulation within the planning system being relaxed to the point where growth-dependent planning cannot be fully effective in delivering widely spread benefits. But this is often a governmental response to the vulnerability of the paradigm to the absence of economic growth. This chapter explores these vulnerabilities further, looking both to the short and longer term. It also examines how the planning system generally responds through offering leverage of private sector development and the problems that current austerity budgets in the public sector pose to this apparent solution in an economic downturn.

The core assumption of economic growth

The main strength and also weakness of the growth-dependent approach lies in its reliance on economic growth to drive urban development activity. Without demand for the new land uses, the growth-dependent model does not work. Demand drives the profitability of new developments, without which the development would not go ahead and the social and environmental benefits, both direct and indirect, cannot be financed. The expectation of growth has not been an unreasonable assumption. Since the postwar period, governments have become accustomed to national economic output increasing. Over the period from the first quarter of 1955 to the last quarter of 2010, it increased in real terms (that is, allowing for inflation) by 3.68 times, that is, an average annual growth rate of 2.4 per cent per annum. This is clearly illustrated in Figure 4.1, which shows the real level of national economic output or GDP. Growth is thus, in some sense, a norm.

However, looking at GDP figures more closely highlights that this growth has not been a steady and continuous upward trajectory. The growth rate has varied up and down. In the year to the first quarter of 1973 it reached almost as high as a heady 10 per cent. But there have also been years, sometimes periods of several years, when growth has been negative, that is, the economy has been in recession. In 1955/56 and 1957/58, national output (quarter to quarter) declined in real terms, but the more serious postwar periods of downturns have been in the early 1970s, the early 1980s, the early 1990s and the period since 2008.

In the early 1970s the economy was tipped into recession by the oil price shocks consequent on the Arab–Israeli war of 1973, the temporary closure of the Suez Canal and the response of a cartel

Figure 4.1: Changing level of economic output, 1955 to 2012, UK: GDP measured quarterly, 2008 prices as at May 2012

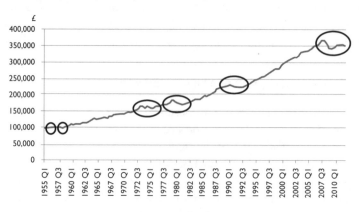

⬭ Periods with years of negative economic growth

Source: ONS, available at: www.ons.gov.uk/ons/index.html

of oil-producing countries in restricting supply. This set in train a severe property crash as a period of oversupply of commercial property was brought catastrophically to an end by the mix of cost inflation, substantial interest rate increases and the fall in demand from occupiers. As many financial institutions had invested heavily in commercial property, this had repercussions across the economy. Annual changes in GDP were negative throughout 1974 and 1975, reinforced by the reductions in government expenditure required by the International Monetary Fund in exchange for emergency finance.

The next decade saw annual GDP fall from the first quarter of 1980 for four successive quarters and not achieve early 1980 levels again until the beginning of 1983. This was a different kind of recession largely associated with the economic shifts engineered by Thatcherite policies. These included the closure of large-scale coal mining, following a bruising battle with the National Union of Mineworkers, the move to natural gas for electricity production (the 'Dash for Gas'), and major de-industrialisation associated with the shift to services. The financial services were particularly significant within this shift after the deregulation in the City of London, known as the 'Big Bang' in 1986 that gave the UK financial markets a considerable international competitive edge. This restructuring supported a decade of uninterrupted growth until the early 1990s when the decision of the UK to leave the European Monetary Union led to GDP falling from the end of 1990 to the middle of 1992. However, the annual falls in GDP were less in this period (2.2 per cent fall at most) compared to the 4 per cent annual fall in the mid-1980s and 3 per cent in early 1974.

All these periods of economic decline were arguably significantly less severe than that being experienced now. From the third quarter of 2008, annual real GDP fell for six successive quarters; between the second quarter of 2008 and the fourth quarter of 2009, the size of national output fell by 5 per cent in real terms. At the time of writing, just after the 2013 Budget, the Office for Budget Responsibility has revised its forecast for GDP growth in 2013 from 1.2 per cent down to 0.6 per cent. The source of this recession lies in two debt crises and the response that is restricting the flow of money into the economy and thus prolonging the downturn.

In 2008, a number of banks worldwide faced major problems with their balance sheets as loans that they had advanced for property purchase and complicated debt instruments that they had invested in (which repeatedly bundled up and then split up batches of high-risk mortgages and debts) were down-valued. The high levels of indebtedness of households through substantial mortgages and consumer debt (for example, credit cards) were suddenly seen as unsustainable rather than a source of ongoing profit to the banks. Several banks needed substantial public sector financial support to return to a semblance of viability. They then proved very reluctant to lend again to households and businesses, leading to the credit crunch.

From 2010 it became apparent that many governments were also in debt to an extent that the financial sector decided was unsustainable. Several European national governments found it increasingly difficult to sell bonds, that is, the debt instruments that governments sell to raise finance. The interest rates that had to be charged to attract buyers for such bonds rose to over 7 per cent in some cases. This meant, of course, that these governments were going to have to pay out substantial amounts in interest just at a point when their budgets were already considered over-indebted. The response demanded by global financial markets and institutions comprised 'austerity' budgets, constraining the amount the public sector could put into the economy to promote growth. The possibility that some countries in Europe, such as Greece, might have to leave the Euro common currency system in order to resolve their budgetary and economic problems through currency devaluation presented a further threat to moving out of recession.

These economic conditions clearly set an important context for government policy, including planning policy. They emphasise that governments had a rationale for basing their planning of urban change on the foundation of economic growth; such growth has been a feature of postwar Britain. However, it is not a reliable foundation. Especially since the 1970s, governments have had to cope with variability in growth rates and years of negative growth. Figure 4.2 shows how the different governments since the 1970s have each faced economic ups and downs.

Figure 4.2: Changing level of economic growth, 1971 to 2012, UK: %
annual change in GDP, quarter on quarter, 2008 prices as at May 2012

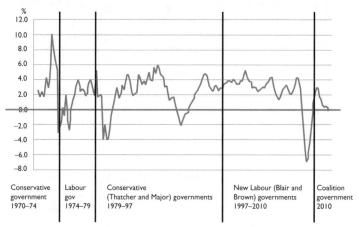

Source: ONS, available at: www.ons.gov.uk/ons/index.html

During upturns, the orientation of a planning system towards growth can seem entirely appropriate, a fortuitous combination of economic circumstances with a policy approach that sees growth-impelled development as delivering in the public interest. Funding social and environmental benefits from development is not really problematic during these upturns. However, in downturns the situation alters and the economic engine of growth can no longer be relied on. In other times and other countries, the response to the failure of the market-led economy to deliver on planning policy goals has led to a greater direct involvement by the state instead. However, as the above discussion has made clear, since the 1970s UK governments have chosen to react to economic downturns by entrenching the growth-dependent paradigm more firmly and loosening regulation that might be thought to discourage it.

So while it might be reasonable – based on past experience – to expect positive average growth rates over the longer term, this cannot be assured in the short or even medium term. There is considerable variation in the amount of economic growth occurring from year to year, and the postwar period has seen several clusters of years when annual growth is negative and economic output falls. One response to this would be just to wait out the downturn, in the expectation that the upturn will arrive and that the growth-dependent model of planning can be restored. The difficulty with this approach is that it may take some considerable time for a downturn to become an upturn; it implies putting any form of more pro-active planning on hold in these periods between upturns.

Spatial patterns of economic growth

Given that urban development is inherently locational, the national economic outlook will be only part of the picture. The spatial distribution of economic growth and of the recovery from economic decline will also be significant. The spatial impacts of recessions depend to some extent on the reasons for the downturn so that industrial restructuring has a different spatial pattern than the effects of a financial crisis. But this is against a strong regional pattern of economic activity across the country. Figure 4.3 shows the regional distribution of per capita contribution to economic activity. This highlights the leading role of the London and the Greater South East area within national economic growth and the lagging position of the North East particularly, but closely followed by the rest of the Northern and Midlands regions.

Figure 4.4 reinforces this message with data on per capita births of new enterprises, giving an idea of regional variations in future economic growth. Again, London and the South East stand out as having high rates of company births. In 2002 the East and South West regions also featured well, with the Eastern region registering above-average rates in 2009. The Northern and Midlands regions again remain in below-average positions.

This means that the turning of any economy cycle is likely to come first in and around London and the South East. Other locations will only experience the upturn in a series of ripple effects outwards from this economic centre. And those locations that are in the most peripheral economic locations may have to wait years for any ripple effect, and then experience the extremely weak echoes of the economic upturn that started in the South East. These economically peripheral locations are not exactly coincident with

Figure 4.3: Regional output, 2009: headline workplace-based Gross Value Added per head Index

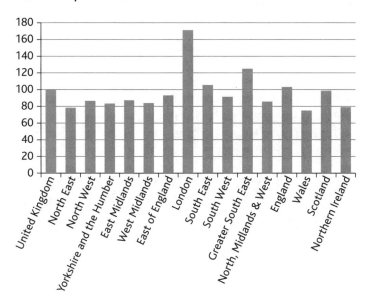

Source: ONS, *Regional Trends,* Table A(1)(i)

being geographically peripheral given the importance of transport infrastructure in linking locations; better linked locations will be better placed to take advantage of the economic upturn beginning in the South East. Thus, while waiting and being ready for the upturn may be one strategy for growth-dependent planners to follow, it will not be effective across spatial locations.

There is an argument that markets should adjust to such shifts – short term or long term – in demand so as to encourage a new round of investment in geographical areas experiencing depressed market conditions. In particular it has been argued that spatial differences in economic conditions would result, eventually, in movements of finance from areas that are experiencing rising prices and almost-full employment of resources, such as labour and land, to those with stable or falling prices. If areas of such relatively lower priced land and labour attracted investment, this would, over time, equalise economic

Figure 4.4: Regional birth of new enterprises, 2009: numbers per 10,000 of adult population

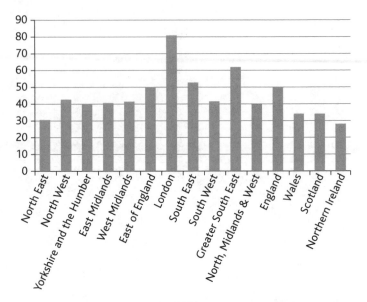

Source: ONS, *Regional Trends,* Table E(1)(ii)

activity across geographical areas. There tends to be some movement of investment and associated urban development in response to the opportunities presented by lower-valued land, costs and wages. However, there also seem to be considerable pressures preventing the spatial equalisation of economic activity within countries.

Under an industrialised society, low-income areas would be more likely to attract industrial development, due to the prospect of cheaper labour. However, this is less relevant today given that manufacturing is less significant within the national economy, and that cheap labour may not be a sufficient attractor for inward employment-generating investment, particularly when compared to cheap labour sources overseas. Industry may be more concerned with the skills as opposed to the costs of labour and also driven by the demands of their management for a location that meets their residential aspirations. With the shift towards a service economy (and manufacturing now accounts for only 11 per cent of output and 8 per cent of employment),[1] low-income communities may not be a major draw. Some services will be looking for a skilled workforce just like industry, while other services – such as personal, retail and leisure services – will be influenced by local demand for their services more than an available workforce. This will draw these service activities to areas of high economic demand rather than pools of cheap labour.

In addition, the attitudes of key economic actors towards risk can result in investment favouring established and demonstrated opportunities for reaping profits, and put a risk premium on untried paths. Firms and investors seem to have strong path dependencies that result in investment going into areas where there has been investment before rather than trying out new paths. These problems are exacerbated by a pattern of economic investment, particularly in property and urban development that favours consumer-led economic activity – based in the housing, retail, distribution and leisure markets – and driven by higher incomes, rather than production-led activity, as with factories and workshops.

Turning to the operation of land markets specifically, economic theory suggests that in circumstances of differential development pressure, over time, land markets will adjust. In areas of low demand, market processes will bring land prices down and this should, eventually, enable developers to make profits again as the gap between land prices and the value of new developments widens again. However, there are reasons to suggest that this may not happen so readily.

Landowners are often resistant to downward movement in land prices, a feature that has been referred to as land markets being 'downwardly sticky'. It may be that the demand for new development is so low that land prices would have to fall considerably, and this is likely to reduce land transactions almost completely rather than prompt development activity. Land values may even fall to negative values if there are remediation costs involved in bringing the land into a state ready for development. This can be the case in former industrial areas where there is a heritage of land contamination. And finally, the uncertainty inherent in a depressed property market and falling land market may be such as to deter developers from getting involved;

they may prefer to wait until the market has apparently bottomed out rather than be the first mover in such an unstable market.

For all these reasons, markets may not adjust readily and easily to a new situation of lower economic growth and reduced market demand so as to promote urban change through new development. Therefore, alternative modes of planning to growth dependence will be necessary.

Coping with economic restructuring

A more profound problem with the growth-dependent model is posed if the decline in economic fortunes that is affecting the profitability of new development is rooted in more extensive economic restructuring rather than the periodic ups and downs of the economic cycle.

There is some debate about the nature of such structural change. The idea first put forward by Kondratiev for a longer but regular cycle in economic fortunes of 50-60 years is not fully accepted by economists.[2] However, there are a number of economic theorists who have analysed the change associated with periods of devaluation of capital in long downturns that then create the conditions for a new wave of investment. Some have associated this with the introduction of new technologies. Schumpeter identified waves of creative destruction in which existing capital is devalued so that investment will occur in the new technologies of the time.[3] Marxists, such as David Harvey, see these as necessary crises of capitalism that pave the way for further rounds of accumulation. Harvey particularly pointed to the way that capital has moved in and out of the built environment as part of a response to crises of over-production or under-consumption of goods and services.[4] However, whether crisis necessarily turns into a period of positive growth and over what timescale remains uncertain.

This is particularly the case if the argument is set in the context of shifting economic power on a global scale, in which capital accumulation and investment are becoming concentrated in new geographic locations. It could be argued that we are currently approaching or are within such a major global economic shift. The dominance of the UK, as the first industrial nation, and the so-called developed countries of Europe and North America, seems to be under challenge. The acronyms of BRIC and CIVET describe new clusters of countries that are experiencing higher growth rates and on a rapid upward trajectory of economic activity. BRIC covers Brazil, Russia, India and China; CIVET covers the next set of emerging countries of Cambodia, Indonesia, Vietnam, Egypt and Turkey. South Africa can appear as the 'S' on the end of either acronym.

The impact of global economic restructuring towards these countries can be seen in recent economic data. World Bank data in 2012[5] suggested that the world economy may be moving into a slow recovery with global growth rates of 2.5 per cent, but this average hides a divergence between lower-income economies, which are forecast to grow by 5.3 per cent, and higher-income countries, where growth will only be 1.4 per cent. So, on the one hand, there are countries such as China and India with growth rates of around 7.6 and 5.3 per cent respectively (although these are both a fall on previous rates) and, on the other, there is predicted growth of about 2 per cent in Japan and the US, while in the Eurozone the situation is one of continued shrinkage, of 0.3 per cent in 2012. Even Germany, one of the strongest economies within Europe, was expected to grow by only 0.7 per cent in 2012.

This puts countries such as the UK in a completely new situation. Instead of being among the leaders of world economic growth, it is potentially moving into the category of laggard in terms of rates of growth, and even being usurped by other countries in terms of being among the world's largest economies. The apparently shorter-term crisis since 2008 may just be a precursor to this new situation. There is a real question as to what a UK economy restructured in new global circumstances might look like. The years to 2008 saw a dramatic increase in the financial services sector, particularly in terms of exports (a vital measure in a globalised world). Financial services exports grew from US$20 billion in 2002–05 to US$72 billion in 2007; in 2009, after the crisis broke, they were still US$53 billion.[6] But can these financial and other services form the basis of a restructured economy? In a rather Panglossian argument, Evan Davis puts particular emphasis on growth in services, particularly education and industries that create intellectual property. But, as even he acknowledges, this will create problems in terms of transition – 'All economic transitions are disorienting; they have winners and losers as new skills become more highly valued' (p 197) – and equality of opportunity – 'The lesson is simple: an economy built on intellectual property is a tough place for people with little intellectual property to sell' (p 195).

This discussion suggests that lower economic growth rates, even once the UK moves into an economic upturn, may be the dominant economic situation for much of the country for some time, and this puts considerable limitations on the ability of growth-dependent planning to deliver desired urban change. The level of demand for new developments may just not be sufficient to make such development profitable and hence allow social and environmental benefits to be negotiated. And there will be losers as well as any winners when growth does return; it will not necessarily reach all.

Another structural shift that may reinforce these changed economic circumstances arises from the demographic trends evident in the UK and many other European countries. This relates to the ageing of the UK population. National statistics[7] suggest that the proportion of the population aged 65 years and over will increase from 17 per cent in 2010 to 24 per cent by 2051. By that date, men will be living almost 26 years after formal retirement and women over 28 years. This has implications for the detail of urban planning, since there will be a need to make towns and cities more elder-friendly. But there will also be economic consequences.

These trends mean that whereas there were 3.2 people of working age for each pensioner in 2010, this is likely to fall to 2.9 in 2051. This figure assumes an increase in the age at which the state pension can be received; without this adjustment, the figure for 2051 would be 2.0. The UK population experienced an increase in fertility rate from 1.63 in 2001 to 2.00 in 2010, but overall it has remained below the replacement rate (to ensure that the population replaces itself in the long term) since 1973. Immigration is the only demographic counter-pressure to this ageing of the UK population, and it currently stands at just over 200,000 per annum over 2006–10.

However, in-migration is likely to respond to the changing economic fortunes of the UK and the continuation of past trends cannot be assumed. Certainly migration is likely to be disproportionately attracted to the more economically buoyant geographical regions, such as London and the South East. This may accentuate the spatial differences in development markets – and hence the potential for growth-dependent planning – in the more as compared to the less prosperous regions.

But even allowing for such in-migration, the UK population is going to be older, and this is likely to mean less disposable income per household. People generally experience a drop in income on retirement and, given the current extent to which many people are under-pensioned, this could be substantial for many households. Unless people stay in the labour market for longer, a drop in aggregate demand in the economy can be expected, and this will be reflected in lower growth rates. Economists are (as ever) rather sanguine about these demographic trends, suggesting the negative impact will be modest but, nevertheless, they are likely to reinforce the shifts arising from the global restructuring of economic production activities.[8]

Leveraging private sector development

These temporal and spatial variations in market demand for new development create a problem in the context of growth-dependent planning and the associated absence of direct public sector development. The response within the UK planning system has been to recognise the necessity at times of leveraging private sector development in specific locations, in effect to pump-prime local property markets so that the conditions in which growth-dependent planning is effective can be (re)established.

As Figure 4.5 illustrates, where the level of market demand depresses the value of the completed development, this may not be enough to cover land and development costs and provide a level of development profit that would be acceptable to a developer. Attempts may be made to negotiate the land price down in order to shift value from the landowner to the developer, but the landowner may not be willing to accept a lower price or the land may have already been purchased at a historic price that renders current development activity insufficiently profitable. In these circumstances, landowners and developers will often sit out the market downturn and wait for more profitable times to return. However, in pursuit of the broader social benefits associated with the development, growth-dependent planners may seek to provide a subsidy to development, a form of gap-funding. Such gap-funding can come in a variety of forms: direct financial grant, cheap land or publicly-funded (at least in part) infrastructure.

A major example of this approach is the linking of the subsidised development of the 2012 Olympic Games site in East London with redevelopment of the immediate area and the regeneration of the wider locality. Here, a major brownfield area of 2.5 square kilometres east of Hackney Wick and west of Stratford town centre was developed by the Olympic Delivery Authority with facilities for the Games including sports venues and housing for the athletes and the creation of a landscaped park. The immediate aim was to create a venue to fulfil the function of hosting the six-week long Olympic and Paralympic sports festival. But essential to the case for this area of London hosting the Games – both to the International Olympic Committee and domestically within the UK – was the argument that there would be longer-term regeneration of the area.

Thus the housing built to accommodate the athletes is now available for other housing needs, the park – a secure and bounded

Figure 4.5: Leveraging private development

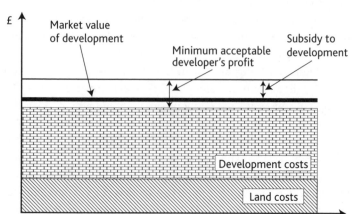

site during the Games – will become a landscaped leisure resources open to Londoners more generally, and some of the venues will become longer-term community sporting facilities. In conjunction with local authority plans for creating 'Stratford City', this is intended to transform perceptions of this part of East London so that businesses and households will be attracted to the area, leading to a virtuous cycle of local economic development. The location of the major Westfield Shopping Centre at Stratford Station (and at an entry to the Games site) can be seen as an example of future investments to come. An Olympic Park Legacy Company, now reconstituted as a Mayoral Development Corporation, the London Legacy Development Corporation, will complete this task.

All this is, however, only possible because of the scale of investment that has gone into the area. Costing the Olympic Games investment is an activity fraught with difficulties, but it is generally accepted that the budget amounted to around £9.3 billion. Of this, £1.7 billion was allocated to regeneration activities and £5.3 billion for buildings and infrastructure. A major element of this was extensive expenditure on cleaning up the contamination and pollution on the site, including remediation of some 1.4 million cubic metres of soil through five 'soil hospitals' or soil-washing machines and the cleansing of the water in the River Lea that runs through the site. Preparation of the site for the 'Big Build' also included demolition of 200 buildings and the more-or-less complete replacement of the utility networks for water, gas, electricity and telecommunications.

But it should also be recognised that there was major investment in the area prior to the Games, and this also constitutes part of the way that local development was leveraged.[9] For example, transport infrastructure serving the area has been transformed. In the early 1980s, Stratford station was served by the Central line on the underground system and a mainline railway line out of Liverpool Street. With the development of the London Docklands in the later 1980s, including Canary Wharf directly to the south, the station also became a terminus for the Docklands Light Railway. Since then further public transport lines have gone through Stratford: the extension to the Jubilee line from Charing Cross through Westminster and along the south side of the Thames before crossing back into

Docklands; the creation of new overground railway lines serving inner north-east London from a mix of existing, unused and new lines; and, probably most importantly, the decision to take High Speed 1, the improved Channel Tunnel rail link, under the Thames and into central London from the east, with a stop at Stratford so that the journey from there to King's Cross takes only 6 minutes.

Lastly there is the management of land in and around the Olympic Park for future development. The development of the athletes' village, comprising 2,818 flats, was supposed to be fully funded by the private sector in anticipation of onwards sales. This did not work out and the public sector had to fund their construction. They are now intended to become a mix of social and private sector housing. Just under half are to be owned and managed as affordable housing by Triathlon Homes and the remaining units have been acquired by a consortium of Delancey and Qatare Diar (a sovereign wealth fund) for onward sale, together with a plot for developing another 2,000 dwellings. It is reported that this sale has been at a loss of £275 million. Certainly the House of Commons Committee of Public Accounts recognised that the public sector was carrying substantial financial risk in 2008:[10] 'The final cost to the public sector will depend on the proceeds arising from the disposal of assets after the Games, in particular, the sale of land on the Olympic Park, as well as the share of profits expected once the Village is converted into housing and sold' (p 3).

The aim is also to construct some 8,000 further dwellings on a number of sites in the vicinity, of which about half will be at affordable rents or prices. Plans exist for five of these, amounting to some 6,800 dwellings. These are known as: Chobham Manor (960 units), East Wick (887 units), Sweetwater (651 units), Marshgate Wharf (2,665 units) and Pudding Mill Lane (1,709 units). If the regeneration works, then private sector development should be profitable and land may even be released at a profit to the London Legacy Development Corporation handling the legacy. However, if market demand does not pull these sites into development, then the Development Corporation has the option of passing these sites on to developers at a lower price. This would be another form of public subsidy, seeking to leverage in private sector finance. That such land price subsidies may be needed is indicated by the decision of Greenwich Peninsular Regeneration Ltd to sit on a site in the area with planning permission dating from 2002 for 1,350 homes rather than build it out in current market conditions. House price differentials between the Stratford area and the London average do not yet seem to have closed as a result of the Games investment.[11]

Whatever public sector resources are being brought to bear – and the Olympic Games is probably an extreme example – there will be an eventual limit to what can be achieved by such leverage of private investment by public funds. It is in the nature of such gap-funding that it is most effective in situations that are not that far from those where market rationality would work anyway. They are a way of adjusting profit at the margin. Any attempt to replace that market rationality would be exceedingly expensive and unlikely to deliver the additional side-benefits that the growth-dependent model promises. Public subsidy may make a particular development happen but, in conditions of persistent low market demand, it will not generate sufficient profitability for planning gain and nor will it lead to the multiplier and spillover effects that this model hopes for.

Furthermore, for leverage planning to be at all effective, it requires considerable public sector funding. This is problematic at present as public sector budgets are currently constrained by the austerity approach being adopted by many domestic governments worldwide, including the UK. This is not just a domestic political decision (although it is important to remember that it *is* a political choice) but is also a result of the reactions of international financial markets. Such markets have seen government deficits as a reason to assess government bonds (IOUs sold by governments to the financial sector) as more risky and therefore to downgrade the credit rating of national governments. Since governments have to sell such bonds to raise the finances needed to cover their expenditure (including, ironically, interest payments on debt previously sold), then such reassessments can be quite threatening. The UK, in particular, given the financial importance of the City of London, is highly dependent on the pound sterling being seen as a safe currency that can be used as a basis of trading and investment. In addition, government tax receipts are constrained by the lack of growth itself (reducing income and corporation taxation receipts while the benefits bill grows) and the fall in revenue from North Sea oil production.

Government fiscal plans are, therefore, extremely tight. Some areas – such as the National Health Service (NHS) – have been protected, resulting in an even tighter squeeze elsewhere. The 2010 Spending Review was committed to cuts totalling £203 billion over four years.[12] The cumulative cuts to the Department for Communities and Local Government's budget (that is, the government department responsible for planning, housing and local government) are forecast to reach 70 per cent by 2018. Finance is being directed towards major infrastructure projects but these will be balanced to some extent by cuts in Whitehall expenditure available, say, for leverage development in other ways.[13] These financial constraints set the context for local government efforts to put money into low-income areas.

While there are debates raging at present about the point at which there should be a move from austerity-based budgeting to using government spending as a stimulus to growth, this is only a marginal shift. It may provide some resources for specific regeneration or infrastructure investment projects, but not enough for public sector resources to be the single most important driver of urban change. The reality is that the private development sector will retain its pivotal role, and this is largely accepted by political parties of all colours and persuasions. This puts the growth-dependence agenda even more firmly centre-stage.

This chapter has looked at the assumption of a sufficiency of economic growth to drive urban development that underpins the growth-dependent planning paradigm, and questioned whether this was a reasonable assumption on which to base planning action. There will always be places and times when and where this paradigm cannot work due to a lack of private sector interest. The current extended period of low growth, dipping in and out of recession, is likely to extend the places where this applies. The global restructuring of economic activity and future demographic change will reinforce this point, and there seems little prospect of public sector spending being able to rectify these short, medium and longer-term economic shifts. This reinforces the need to find an alternative paradigm for effective planning.

FIVE

The environmental and social consequences of growth-dependent planning

This chapter provides a different critique of growth-dependent planning to that provided in the last chapter. It looks to the consequences of pursuing this approach in terms of environmental sustainability and social impacts. It begins by setting out and then critiquing the argument that promoting new development can be a pathway to greener growth. Following this, the chapter then considers the way that growth-dependent planning operates through achieving uplift in land values, and discusses the consequences for urban areas and local communities. In doing so it sets this in the context of existing inequalities within urban areas as both a source of the profitability of market-led development and a consequence of the uneven impacts of such development.

Growth-dependent planning as green growth

The growth in interest in the sustainability of urban areas generally and urban development specifically has put a new slant on the growth-dependent planning model.[1] Sustainability, as has often been noted, is a highly contested term. It is broadly used to indicate characteristics of activities that have economic and also social and environmental benefits. Because of the recent saliency of the environmental agenda – covering climate change, biodiversity loss, soil degradation, loss of flood protection and the health impacts of air, land and water pollution – attention has particularly been paid to how environmental benefits can go alongside the pursuit of economic activity. This has led to an approach termed green growth or ecological modernisation.[2] The aim here is to pursue economic development pathways that will lead to lower environmental burdens through the use of cleaner technologies and associated behavioural change. The ideal is the identification of market niches that target the green consumer so that environmental protection becomes a source of profits.

While originally intended to guide national governments in developing their economic strategies, such green growth has also become an attractive idea for guiding local economic development and setting the parameters for planning urban development and change.[3] More environmentally aware growth-dependent planning searches for the various ways that attracting investment into an area and generating new urban development can assist in long-term environmental protection. There are a number of different aspects to this argument.

First, there is the potential for new development to be at considerably higher environmental standards compared to existing buildings and places. This has particularly been applied to energy efficiency but also other features such as water efficiency, the handling of surface drainage and biodiversity features. Through new development, it is argued, urban areas can be incrementally upgraded to produce a radical shift in the environmental sustainability of the built environment. In the UK current policy is for all new housebuilding to be zero-carbon by 2016[4] and all new non-domestic development by 2019. This is being achieved through a mix of local planning policy and enhanced regulation at planning permission and building consent stages. On this logic, the more development that occurs and the larger the areas that are being developed or re-developed, the quicker this transition to a more sustainable urban future will occur.

Second, it is possible to conceive of planning gain being used specifically for environmental ends. For example, this could include the allocation of part of a development site for a nature area or the funding of such a nature conservation area off-site. Or again, under the proposed guidance on how to assess whether a development attains zero-carbon status, there is a provision for developers to install renewable energy technology onsite or to fund energy efficiency improvements and renewable energy generation capacity off-site.[5] Effectively the contribution to carbon reductions off-site can be included in the calculation of the carbon efficiency of the development itself.

And third, there is the possibility that urban development could contribute to the broader restructuring of local and national economies by providing demand for the eco-technology involved in urban construction processes and the management and operation of buildings. This would cover a whole range of products and services, from water-saving showerheads to facilities management consultancy. Whether building more environmentally sustainable developments will in practice create a greener national economy, let alone local economic development that is oriented around such eco-technology, is a moot point. Clearly this could favour industries importing building materials and green technologies. But as part of a broader industrial strategy – whether national, regional or local – it is clearly a possibility and a possibility that does not emerge without substantial sustainable urban development to create the demand.

During his tenure as mayor at the Greater London Authority, Ken Livingstone explored the possibility of creating a hydrogen economy for London. This would involve shifting key energy demands, particularly from the transport sector, towards hydrogen fuel cells and furthermore, building a local economic development strategy around innovation using this technology. While there were concerns raised about public acceptance, safety and economic viability, this was a bold attempt to marry growth-dependent planning with an ecological modernisation approach. Some urban development initiatives – such as the creation of ecoparks – seek literally to build a green growth industrial strategy into the development.[6] In such ecoparks, not only is the estate built to a high environmental standard, but every effort is made to ensure that the waste products (materials, water, heat) from one industrial or commercial occupier can be used as an input into another occupier.

The most recent relevant exposition of the green growth argument can be found in the NPPF.[7] This attempts to set its enthusiastic espousal of the growth-dependent paradigm within a broader sustainable development agenda. In doing so, it relies on a tripartite definition of sustainable development, encompassing economic and also social and environmental dimensions (p 2). The environmental role is defined as: 'contributing to protecting and enhancing our natural, built and historic environment; and, as part of this, helping to improve biodiversity, use natural resources prudently, minimise waste and pollution, and mitigate and adapt to climate change including moving to a low carbon economy' (p 2).

In line with the green growth arguments, the NPPF expresses the hope that the economic, social and environmental dimensions are 'mutually dependent', and that 'Economic growth can secure higher social and environmental standards' (p 3). It thus charges the planning system with seeking gains on all three dimensions 'jointly and simultaneously' (p 3). As examples of how these synergies could be achieved, it suggests the following:

- enabling job creation within urban areas and villages;
- achieving net gains for nature as a result of urban development;
- replacing poor design with better design within the built environment;
- improving people's living conditions; and
- widening the choice of high quality homes.

The next section, however, highlights the tensions and challenges that this approach implies.

The implications for environmental sustainability

There are a number of ways in which a growth-led approach, even a green growth approach, raises concerns from a sustainability perspective. The most fundamental is about resource use. Clearly this approach relies heavily on new development as the engine of urban change, and such development inevitably involves the use of resources. Construction processes use energy and water directly, but by far the greatest use of resources is represented by the materials used. In some cases, as with marble, sand or aggregates, the material is a natural resource. In other cases, as with steel or concrete, the material is manufactured from natural resources. Most of these resources are stock resources that are not renewed on anything other than a geological timescale. Timber is an exception here, being a renewable resource that is heavily used in construction in some countries. Where the building materials are manufactured and/or transported large distances, there are associated energy and carbon costs. If the energy involved in transporting building materials is added to that for manufacturing them, then a figure for the embodied carbon of the materials is derived, a further indicator of the environmental impact of urban development processes.

Drawing attention to the environmental impact of the new development promoted by growth-dependent planning raises the question of whether there should be limits imposed on the overall quantum of urban development from an environmental perspective. Does it makes sense to rely on a planning approach that encourages large-scale development, including redevelopment based in many cases on the demolition and disposal of existing built assets?

However, there is another perspective, one that emphasises the potential for reducing the environmental impact of new development through a variety of measures. For example, construction techniques using renewable resources can be prioritised. Timber has already been mentioned, but designers are working with natural materials such as hemp, straw and lime in an effort to increase the proportion of renewable resources within a building. The BRE Innovation Park houses a 'natural house', promoted by the Prince's Trust.[8] This is built in traditional style and using conventional methods, but with natural materials including a single skin of aerated clay block, with lime-based render and plaster, and insulation using compressed wood fibre and sheep's wool. Roof tiles are clay and all floors and windows are made from FSC-certified timber. Timber is also being explored as a possibility for commercial and medium-rise buildings. This involves engineered as opposed to cut timber, where multiple thin layers of timber are cross-laminated together to provide enhanced structural properties as well as fire resistance and energy efficiency. There are an increasing number of examples of the application of this technology.[9]

Another approach is to design developments so as to be 'lean', making less use of materials. Here developments can be planned to be much more efficient in terms of the resources used. Reducing the weight of constructions while maintaining their engineering integrity and robustness means that less resources are used for the same functionality of the building.[10] Furthermore, recycling of materials within the construction industry allows the greater re-use of materials, particularly after the demolition of buildings. To some extent this already happens with bricks and other elements of architectural heritage value. However, this tends to be limited to historic buildings and the desire to retain key features of a building or an urban area in the name of conservation. The problem is that use of such salvaged materials is often more expensive as it requires specific labour input to recover the materials in a condition that allows their re-use.

More recently methods of analysis have been developed that allow consideration of the embodied carbon of an existing built structure.[11] As indicated above, embodied carbon refers to the carbon arising from energy used in the production and transportation of a building material. For conventional bricks, this embodied carbon is high as substantial temperatures are needed to fire the brick. Knowing the embodied carbon of all materials would enable developments to be designed so as to use materials that have lower embodied carbon, replacing elements on a like-for-like basis but with a carbon saving or, more radically, redesigning a building so that it can make greater use of low carbon options. Since the travel costs of getting materials to site is a significant part of embodied carbon, strategies that prioritise the use of relatively local materials can also reduce the environmental impact of design.

Integrating a concern with embodied carbon into refurbishment projects can also support decision making about whether to conserve those existing elements within the building that have the highest embodied carbon and to design any new building so as to incorporate these as far as possible. Thus, for example, an existing office block would not be completely demolished to facilitate redevelopment but the concrete shell (which has a high level of embodied carbon) could be conserved and the new development built around it.

A focus on the energy and carbon costs of building new development raises the question as to whether the full energy and carbon costs of the resources involved in the building materials used and the construction process outweigh the energy and carbon savings of a greener development design, including enhanced energy efficiency and use of low carbon energy (electricity and heat). The answer to this question depends heavily on the assumed lifespan of a new development. The more rapidly that buildings come to the end of their economic life span and are redeveloped, the greater the likelihood of embodied energy and carbon costs exceeding operational energy and carbon savings; and conversely, the longer that a building can be used, perhaps moving across different kinds of use through flexibility of building design, then the greater the overall energy and carbon benefits of the development.

Through all these means, the resources, energy and carbon associated with urban development can be reduced. This is essentially an example of the 'Factor Four' or even 'Factor Ten' school of thought, which argues that greater economic output can be achieved with considerably less resource use per unit of output, so that per annum resource use can be radically reduced even as growth is maintained.[12] It suggests the possibility of a good fit with the ideas of green growth or ecological modernisation reviewed above.

However, the ability of such green growth to deliver on its promises depends on the extent to which these shifts in building and urban design and associated construction processes can actually be achieved, and achieved on a significant scale and at a rapid pace. There is scope to use the regulatory powers of the planning regime to achieve this, but the difficulty is that exercising tighter regulatory control to push the boundaries of building and urban design is likely to increase the costs of development. There will be a trade-off between, at the minimum, achieving these environmental efficiencies and generating other social benefits from planning gain on a development. The worst-case scenario – from a growth-dependent perspective – is that the quantum of regulation deters development completely because it has, from the developer's point of view, rendered the project unviable. Thus growth-dependent planning can achieve environmental efficiencies that may go some way to refuting the arguments of environmentalist critics, but it will only do so up to a point – dictated by project viability – and may do so at the expense of other forms of benefit to the community.

More importantly, this emphasis on reducing the environmental impact of new urban development misses three important aspects involved in making the urban environment more sustainable. The first relates to the limited impact that new development can make to the overall built stock. New development amounts to about 1-2 per cent of the existing stock, more in times and locations subject to growth but also less in periods of economic downturn. It is oft-quoted that the over 70 per cent of housing that will exist in 2050 has already been built, some of it a long time ago. A report by Foresight on energy and the built environment emphasised that the UK's built stock is old:[13]

> By 2050, 65-70 per cent of the dwelling stock in existence is likely to have been built before 2000. The non-domestic stock is somewhat more modern than the housing stock. Nevertheless, just over half of all commercial and industrial properties were built before 1940 and only 9 per cent after 1990. Just over a quarter of commercial building space by area was built before 1940 and only 15 per cent since 1990.

A footnote pointed out that 'retail property is disproportionately older with about 40% of the floorspace built almost 70 years ago; about 30% of office floorspace and a quarter of industrial floorspace is this old.' Thus a concern with the environmental impact of the built environment as a whole should centrally consider the existing built stock and the need to retrofit it in order to reduce environmental impacts, particularly to increase energy efficiency and reduce carbon emissions associated with the heating, cooling and use of appliances within buildings.

Considering embodied carbon further throws the emphasis onto the importance of the existing stock. It is not just that these buildings are already there and are likely to be there for a considerable time to come. They represent important environmental resources. Thus, in order to conserve these resources and the associated carbon, it can be argued that the refurbishment and retrofitting of the urban environment should be prioritised rather than promoting clearance and new development or extensive refurbishment as is associated with 'facadism' (development behind a preserved front wall of a building). Growth-dependent planning can be criticised for ignoring the importance of making existing buildings and spaces more sustainable and, more generally, making better use of the resources that are already tied up in existing buildings and urban assets.

Finally, this emphasis on the built stock – whether new built or existing – misses the importance of behaviour as the link between physical artefacts such as buildings and environmental impacts.[14] It is people who use energy, who generate waste and who create pollution. They do so in association with a range of technological and physical elements, but the behavioural dimension is essential. If left dormant, most buildings or other technology do not continue to have such environmental impacts. So planning needs to consider how the built environment is used, and thus engage with residents, businesses and other sectors of local communities in shaping that use.

The difficulty of reconciling a concern over environmental sustainability with the growth-dependent paradigm can be seen in the current NPPF.[15] Attempts to resolve the tensions between the growth-dependent basis of this central government policy document and environmental sustainability through a green growth approach depend on, first, being able to influence the location of new development and, second, on shaping the detailed design of such new developments.

In terms of influencing the location of new development, the NPPF rehearses well-known arguments[16] that such development should be in locations that 'support a pattern of development which, where reasonable to do so, facilitates the use of sustainable modes of transport', such modes meaning public transport as well as cycling and walking (p 9). However, this can readily come into conflict with an approach that relies on the private sector bringing forward sites for development and encourages planners to understand market signals and respond to these in facilitating development. Even allowing for the inclusion of the word 'sustainable' in the presumption in favour of sustainable development, there is a potential, perhaps inevitable, tension here. A growth-dependent paradigm sends out strong signals against deterring market-led development when and where it is proposed by developers, even if this would disrupt an overall pattern of development that is more carbon-efficient in terms of travel and transport.

The way to cut through this Gordian knot would be to use public landownership to influence where urban development occurs, and investment in public transport systems to link development sites so that car dependence is reduced. Neither of these are currently emphasised within the UK planning system, since public landownership plays a very subsidiary role in directing development locations and public sector funding for public transport infrastructure investment is severely limited. It has also been suggested that the provisions in the NPPF permitting the setting of local parking standards may act to undermine the promotion of more energy-efficient modes of travel.

The area where the NPPF may support the planning for more energy and carbon-efficient urban forms is in its encouragement of town centre development. Here a sequential test is to be applied for all town centre land uses – presumably including retail and commercial properties – so that town centres are favoured over edge-of-centre, and edge-of-centre over sites further out. There seems to be a clear synergy perceived between promoting economic growth in town centres and enabling more energy-efficient travel, largely because both can be achieved by concentrating new development in more central locations.

The other route towards reconciling growth dependence and environmental sustainability lies in encouraging specific features of development design and negotiating for these during the regulatory phase when planning permission is granted. The difficulty here is that the NPPF – like other guides to sustainable development design – includes a very long list of desirable features of a development (pp 6-7, but also throughout the NPPF). Where such a long list exists, the potential for trade-offs and discretionary prioritisation of one feature over another also exists. This approach does not ensure that the most resource or carbon-efficient options will be pursued.

As a result of these tensions between environmental sustainability and growth-dependent planning, the statement in the NPPF on the transition to a low carbon economy (p 5) is relatively weak. It recommends that local planning authorities should 'encourage the re-use of existing resources, including conversions of existing buildings and the use of renewable resources such as energy'. This would be considered inadequate by environmentalists concerned with the need to reduce carbon emissions to combat climate change.

Growth-dependent planning as land value uplift

The social consequences of pursuing growth-dependent planning largely arise from the way that this approach is based on the generation of uplift in development and land values.

A reliance on growth-dependent planning means that, in localities where demand for new uses is strong, low value land uses will be at risk of being replaced by higher value uses through redevelopment and refurbishment activity. Indeed these are the ideal circumstances for growth-dependent planning to be effective in that this can allow successful negotiation of planning gain to secure local community benefits. This will be at the expense of the loss of the low-value land uses, but it is the ability to transform those land uses from low to high market value that lies at the core of the profitability of market-led development.

This may not matter; not all low-value land uses are that significant to local communities, and they may welcome the opportunities that come with the economic transformation of their areas. But it may also be the case that some low-value land uses are considered important to the everyday lives of sections of the community, and fulfil an important and irreplaceable function. In these cases, the issue becomes one of protecting lower value uses that are serving these important community needs from replacement with higher value uses that meet the needs of a different group of people, that is, people with the greater purchasing power who would underpin the viability of the new development. Particular problems are created where there is uneven distribution of benefits locally or incremental change.

An example of the former problem would be where an area locating a mix of light industrial SMEs, such as are often found around and under railway lines, becomes a viable proposition for redevelopment, say, with a mix of new uses including offices, high-value retail and flats for sale. The development may generate sufficient profit for a range of community benefits – say, a sports facility and some affordable housing – but this will be of little consolation to the small businesses that lose their affordable workspaces. Here one sector of the local community is benefiting, but at the cost of another.

Incremental change is particularly apparent in tourist areas. Here the facilities that meet the everyday needs for residents – whether for shopping or housing or leisure – can be at risk of being replaced with uses oriented towards the tourist trade – hotels, holiday cottages, different kinds of retail outlet and leisure activities. For example, in Grasmere, a tourist honey-pot in the Lake District, the bakers is now a holiday cottage, the two banks are a gift shop and a café, the greengrocers is another café, the butchers … and so on. The Coop and the post office (inside a chemist and tourist shop) are the only everyday retail facilities. This may create employment for local people, but at the cost of other aspects of everyday life. Local people may find themselves having to travel further for food shopping or a sports facility, travelling which imposes financial and environmental costs. And, of course, loss of housing to the second home or holiday rental market creates considerable problems for local people seeking affordable housing in tourist areas, where demand pushes house prices up.

Another example of incremental change is provided by the change of use of office space to residential use, as is being encouraged by current central government policy (see Chapters 2 and 8). Where the office space is vacant and has been for some time, this could enable unused elements of the built environment to fulfil a social need, particularly where the resulting housing units are priced for the lower-income end of the market. However, such changes of use can also result in existing SME office users being evicted in order to provide higher-income housing. This is the concern about the impact of the current government policy in inner-city areas that have traditionally housed SMEs in small office units above shops, locations that would now be highly desirable residential locations.

The dilemma in such cases is whether the benefits to the local community of the replacement development are sufficient to outweigh the costs, and exactly who within that local community is benefiting and who is losing. This can be difficult to judge, particularly in cases of incremental replacement of land uses as opposed to large-scale projects.

Normally compensation will be offered for the loss of land uses on development, even low value ones. But the question then becomes one of the adequacy of that compensation and, particularly important, who is receiving it. Usually it is the landowner who receives such compensation. In the case of the SMEs, the businesses may only be tenants while their landlords will be the recipients of the compensation. These small businesses will have to look for alternative accommodation, which may be increasingly difficult to find in an area undergoing redevelopment. Even if an owner-occupier receives financial compensation for the loss of housing, say, there may be considerable difficulty in finding replacement accommodation in an area that is experiencing rising land values, a trend accentuated by the impact on the surrounding area of the new development that growth-dependent planning is promoting.

Since the aim of growth-dependent planning is to raise the market value of development in an area, this tends to go hand in hand with gentrification.[17] This term has been coined to refer to the change in social composition of an area over time, either with redevelopment or more incremental refurbishment. The original usage referred to instances in the inner suburbs of cities where housing – that had been in the rental market and in a zone traditionally thought of as transitional – was bought up by middle-income households and small-scale developers and refurbished for occupation or onward sale. Over time, the actions of a few pioneer households and developers became more widespread and the area changed in character, middle-class households replacing lower-income ones and higher-priced owner-occupied housing replacing lower-value rented accommodation.

More generally the term has come to be used to understand the process by which an area of a town or city becomes oriented to the needs and demands of higher-income groups, through the replacement of one type of shop with another, of industrial employment activities with service ones and of lower-value with higher-value property. This, it can be seen, is effectively the rationale of growth-dependent planning. It is deemed to succeed when such uplifts in property values occur with associated change in the sections of the urban population that are catered for by such property. This was seen in the Elephant and Castle case mentioned in Chapter 3, where the whole rationale was to move the area into a different property value category.

The extraction of planning gain can act as a bulwark against such wholesale gentrification, but much depends on how it is used and which sections of the community get to benefit from it. As indicated above, planning gain can be used to bring investment in to finance general local services, such as schools and hospitals, which are available to be used by all local residents. Alternatively, planning gain can be targeted at specific social groups seen as being in particular need, although central government rules do require the community benefit to be both proportionate to the development occurring and to have a planning rationale.[18] Planning gain that is channelled into public landscaping and other improvements to the public realm, while potentially of general benefit to all who use the area, is likely to contribute to the uplift in property values through enhancing the urban environment within which buildings are situated. Thus these forms of community benefit may be more sectional in their impact and actually contribute to gentrification of the area.

Thus it is intrinsic to the growth-dependent model to see rising property values as a positive sign. Indeed the highest accolade that an area subject to growth-dependent planning can achieve is that local people no longer wish for further change or any new development. Thus the much-derided term of NIMBYism can actually be used as a marker of success. Similarly, if an area progresses to the point of receiving protection from further development through conservation designations, then this too can be seen as the limits of successful change having been reached.

There is a difference in impact, though, between smaller-scale development associated with incremental growth in an area and larger-scale development that can potentially transform an area economically and socially. With a small development, there is less scope for the development itself to change the land value landscape of the locality. The profits here tend to come from a change of use from, say, some garages to a group of houses or a row of shops into a small office block. There is also scope for the timing of the development to catch a rising curve of values in a local market, so that the developer benefits from rising development prices by the time the completed buildings are marketed. A new development may then contribute to the continuing upward movement in market prices by continuing the transformation of an area. This would only stop when new developments led to an oversupply of new property.

Thus houses, offices, shops and industrial units will be built in locations where there is demand, land can be found and planning permission granted. But there will be little potential for community benefits if the land price, construction costs and development value leave only sufficient profit to meet the developer's lowest expectations of an adequate return. Planning gain in these cases is likely to be minimal. Where there are set tariffs, these are likely to be factored into development costs and drive down the price that the developer is willing to offer to the landowner. This is the norm for much routine development, where developers make a 'normal' profit in economists' terms and the new buildings largely match those already existing in the locality. The role of planning here is largely to ensure that the new development fits into the locality in terms of character, design and functionality.

On a larger scale, however, there is the scope for development itself to instigate a change in the locality from an area of lower to higher land values, rather than just marginally keeping such a change going, as happens with smaller-scale developments. Town centres can be transformed, docklands turned into leisure hotspots, new office quarters created, new residential areas provided to bring a population, shoppers and businesses into an area. Then the development itself may generate a tsunami of increasing land values in the area. This makes such large developments an attractive economic opportunity for developers able to amass sufficient funds and to operate on such a scale, because the development activity itself will be creating the changes in the local property market that drive development values, and hence the profitability of the scheme, upwards. This is different to the smaller schemes, where the developer's profit relies on the already prevailing property values and the development will make only a marginal difference to prevailing property market movements.

These development strategies, however, only work on any scale provided there is sufficient demand for the development. The larger developments will seek to create that demand by attracting new property buyers – residential and commercial – into an area. The smaller-scale development will usually be dependent on the demand already apparent in the local property markets. However, if that demand – actual or potential – is not realised, then the developments will not be profitable and, after a few clear failures, development activity is likely to dry up. If the level of development activity in a locality is more than sufficient to satisfy all apparent demand – whether local or attracted from other localities – then property values will stall or even go into decline, and further development activity will be deterred. Developments may even stop in mid-construction, and development sites will be mothballed.

These dynamics have considerable implications for the communities in localities subject to development pressures.

The implications for local communities

From the above discussion it can be seen that a planning approach that is dependent on growth may not always be a problem. There will be contexts where development is largely taking the form of infill or small-scale development, improving the area at the margins and perhaps supporting any upward movement in the local property markets. This will be to the presumed benefit of local property owners without imposing too many additional burdens on the local infrastructure. Small amounts of planning gain may be extracted through a tariff system or negotiation on individual applications.

Repeated small-scale development may begin to transform the local property market, creating problems for lower-income local people who wish to enter the housing market for the first time and cumulatively requiring new investment in infrastructure, such as schools. Whether this is problematic depends on the rate of change, the responsiveness of infrastructure agencies and the scope for incorporating affordable housing within the new developments.

Larger-scale development may also prove advantageous in certain circumstances, particularly if it is on greenfield sites or empty brownfield sites. The potential for transformation and the associated land value uplift in such cases can be considerable. Agricultural or industrial land value is likely to be considerably below the land value associated with the completed development. Problems will probably only arise where there are considerable remediation costs involved, as there can be with some industrial sites. Here, public sector funding to deal with site contamination may be required to render a brownfield site a viable development site, unlocking large urban areas for regeneration.

The difficulty comes when a redevelopment project or further smaller-scale development consequent on a major regeneration scheme begins to affect established communities in terms of replacing the land uses that have served those communities.

In such cases, growth-dependent planning is using the replacement of one set of land values by another as the economic basis for redevelopment and any associated planning gain. This will also involve replacement of land uses and may involve the loss of people's houses, or industrial and commercial activity that provides jobs or facilities that serve the local community. Thus in many cases, the development supported and indeed advocated by growth-dependent planning is replacement development, which clearly has a direct impact on those whose homes, workplaces and properties are being replaced. There may be financial recompense, either through the private market or by compulsory purchase, but this will not reflect the full redeveloped value of the sites, since it is essential to the logic of the development process that it does not. These will be lower-value land uses than those proposed by the development scheme, otherwise it would not prove profitable to build.

From the perspective of growth-dependent planning, this land value uplift is a sign of success. However, this uplift may also adversely affect local people, even those who do not directly lose their homes or jobs as a result of the development, because growth, higher demand, inward investment, high land and property values will all be associated with increased costs of living for local communities. Thus even outside the actual development site, land uses will be replaced as development-led growth suggests a market logic for higher-value land uses in the locality over lower-value ones. Shops will go upmarket, houses outside the development site will be worth more and lower-value sites, such as those still in industrial use, will become prime targets for infill redevelopment. This replacement of existing land uses by new development and of lower-value land uses with higher-value ones will inevitably lead to a change in the local community. These economic signals associated with higher-value property and services will attract higher-income residents. Thus the replacement of land uses will also be associated with, to some extent, a replacement of people.

The important context for this discussion is the existing inequality of our society. The usual way of measuring inequality is using the Gini coefficient. This is devised by plotting the distribution of all households against the distribution of all income, and then calculating how far the plotted distribution diverges from a perfectly equal distribution. A Gini coefficient of 1 indicates perfect equality and the lower the figure below 1, the greater the level of societal income inequality. The Gini coefficient for 2006/07 was 34.5%, suggesting significant inequality, although this had improved from 26.7% in 1977. Figure 5.1 illustrates how the Gini coefficient has changed over time since the mid–late 1970s. After a slight increase over 1978 to 1981, the coefficient was largely stable for three years. Then there was another more significant improvement during 1984 to 1990. However, this was followed by a decline from 1990 to 1995/96. Modest increases to 2001/02 were followed by another fall over the next two years.

The problem with the measurement of inequality provided by the Gini coefficient is that it is a broad societal measure that does not distinguish between the relatively richer and poorer groups in society in terms of who is gaining when inequality declines. Figure 5.2 shows the share of different social groups in total disposable income, and this highlights the problem at the extremes of the income scale. Over a quarter, 27 per cent, of disposable income is received by the richest 10 per cent of households, while the poorest 10 per cent receive just 3 per cent of disposable income. The richest 20 per cent of households receive 42 per cent of disposable income and the poorest 20 per cent receive 8 per cent. But the greatest indictment of government policy is that inequality in terms of the different situation of the richest and poorest households has increased. Between 1977 and 2006/07, the share of the poorest 10 per cent of households fell from 4 to 3 per cent. During the same period, the richest 10 per cent of households

Figure 5.1: Income inequality: change in Gini coefficient

Source: www.ons.gov.uk/ons/taxonomy/index.html?nscl=Income+Inequality
+of+Households

Figure 5.2: Income inequality: percentage share of different decile groups

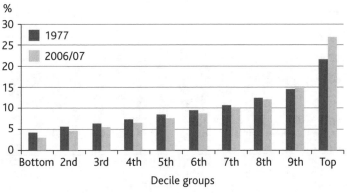

Source: www.ons.gov.uk/ons/taxonomy/index.html?nscl=Income+Inequality
+of+Households

increased their share from 22 to 27 per cent. In this context, the loss of land uses and properties meeting the needs of low-income populations cannot be disregarded.

There is a strong spatial pattern to such inequality. Figure 5.3 shows that household disposable income is above the national average in the London area and the South East and Eastern regions. This echoes the pattern of regional inequality in growth discussed in Chapter 4. However, deprivation can also be found within relatively prosperous regions. As Figure 5.4 shows, the prevailing regional pattern is broadly repeated when considering the percentage of people where their families are dependent on key social benefits (Figure 5.4), but London also has its share of deprivation internally, despite its economic advantages nationally. And there are patterns of inequality on a much finer scale. The End Child Poverty campaign estimate that on average 20 per cent of children live in households earning less than 60 per cent of the median income, but they also identified 69 council wards nationally where more than half the children are in poverty.[19]

Figure 5.3: Regional income inequality, 2009: gross disposable household income, £ per head at current basic prices (index)

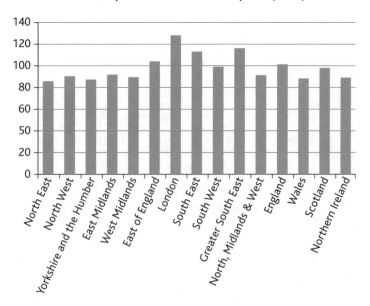

Source: ONS, *Regional Trends,* Table A(4)(ii)

Figure 5.4: Percentage of people within families dependent on key benefits, 2009

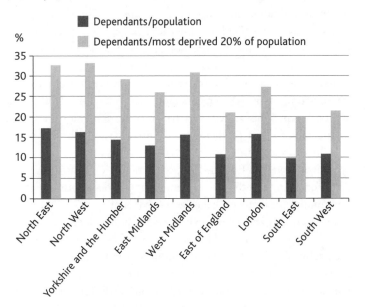

Source: ONS, *Regional Trends,* Table I(2)

Thus the UK is a profoundly unequal country. This is the case even compared with other European countries. As *The Economist* has found:[20]

> Britain has the widest disparities, with average GDP per head in central London more than nine times larger than in parts of Wales. Central London's income per head is inflated by commuters who work in the city but do not live there, but even adjusting for this Britain has a big regional spread.

And it is likely that current changes to the welfare system and the local government finance reforms outlined in Chapter 4 will exacerbate existing socio-spatial inequalities. This sets the context for considering the impact of growth-dependent planning.

There is a solid body of research that has highlighted that growth-dependent strategies are often not effective in benefiting all elements of a local community, indeed, quite the contrary.[21] For example, using a case study of Sheffield, Buckner and Escott considered how far major retail development created job opportunities that local residents could access. They show that 'many residents remain marginalised from local jobs' (p 157). Loftman and Nevin, in a review of the use of 'prestige projects' in urban regeneration, concluded that (p 300): 'the approach represents, at best, a partial and one-dimensional response to the multifaceted problems facing urban areas, and, at worst, a vehicle for exacerbating social polarisation in Britain's cities.' And a systematic review of English-language literature on gentrification by Atkinson found that the effects through household displacement and community conflict have been 'largely harmful' (p 107), going on to point out the gap between the language in policy documentation of positive impacts from local housing and neighbourhood change and the likely effects on the ground: 'the aims of an inclusive renaissance agenda appear to have been discarded in favour of policies which pursue revitalization through gentrification and displacement' (p 107).

One element in the failure of growth-dependent planning to tackle socio-spatial inequalities concerns the multiplier effect of local investment and how this can vary considerably between areas. With some investments in a locality, the initial income generated stays within that locality and circulates among local households and businesses to be spent and reinvested again and, hopefully, again and again. However, with some investments a substantial share of the first round of spending is distributed outside the locality, and this brings the local multiplier effect to a sharp halt. It has been argued in particular that retail development that results in multiples or outlets and subsidiaries of major national and international brands being located in an area results in this rapid outflow of financial resources from an area.

The New Economics Foundation has made a particular study of the multiplier effect of money spent in a locality and the flow of money out of that locality.[22] For example, in a study of local authority procurement in Northumberland, they found that local suppliers re-spent on average 76 per cent of their income in the local area, compared to 36 per cent for suppliers from outside that area. They have developed a methodology called LM3 (the local multiplier 3) as a way of measuring how organisational expenditure or specific initiatives have an impact on the local economy by considering the extent to which expenditure circulates and re-circulates within the locality, or leaks out of it to other areas. Current growth-dependent planning approaches do not distinguish between development on the basis of the extent to which financial flows are kept within the locality.

Another dynamic that is involved in creating and reinforcing these socio-spatial inequalities concerns the treatment of many environmental impacts as externalities by market processes. Environmental externalities refer to features that influence the demand (and in some cases the supply) of goods and services but are not fully captured by the price mechanism, that is, they are not priced.[23] Sometimes aspects are partially captured by land and property prices, but the extent to which this occurs depends on how salient the features are to buyers and sellers of property, particularly in relation to other features of the buildings. There are both positive externalities – as in the case of views of and access to a beautiful landscape – and there are negative externalities – such as proximity to sources of pollution of various sorts.

One feature of the processes by which land uses are sorted between different groups in society is that there appears to be a strong tendency towards environmental injustice in distributive terms.[24] This means that lower-income groups seem to have a greater tendency to be found in locations experiencing negative externalities and wealthier groups in locations benefiting from positive externalities. There are some nuances to this generalisation (as Chapter 6 discusses more fully), but it does seem that market processes create these patterns and, furthermore, reinforce them once they have been established. Wealthier households are able to buy in locations that have more environmental assets and fewer environmental 'bads'; this option is not open to lower-income households.

Growth-dependent planning cannot rectify this distributive environmental injustice since it relies on market processes and signals to promote urban change. Rather, it will reinforce the ability of higher-income groups to buy properties that insulate them to some degree against negative environmental externalities. Indeed, regulation can reinforce market dynamics in creating such inequalities. For example, there may be happenstance in the original location of waste tips near low-income communities, but this can then become embedded by the mix of regulation and market dynamics. Regulation tends to put more land uses with negative externalities in already degraded environments and to be less open to influence from low-income communities, and market processes give more location choice to those with higher incomes, who tend to shy away from locations near waste sites and favour instead sites with positive environmental externalities.[25]

Thus, even if growth-dependent planning is successful in attracting inward investment to an area and community replacement does not occur – assumptions which themselves can be questioned – there are good arguments to suggest that this may not lead to the benefits of that investment being mainly captured in that locality and being felt equally by all social groups there, let alone specifically improving the lot of low-income groups in our highly unequal society.

SIX

Reforming the planning agenda

The previous chapters have outlined the paradigm of growth-dependent planning, indicated how it has become embedded in the British planning system, explored the underlying economic model and laid out a critique in terms of both the underpinning economic assumptions and the social and environmental impact of pursuing such an approach. This and the following chapters set out a response to this analysis, suggesting an alternative approach that could sit alongside growth-dependent planning within a re-balanced planning system.

The argument is that in some local contexts growth-dependent planning may still be the most appropriate paradigm to adopt if local economic conditions allow and if planning is pursued pro-actively through effective regulation and negotiation and with the support of local communities. But in many other situations something else is needed. If this is not recognised, then considerable social and environmental harm can result from poorly regulated market-led development or, as it often the case, local planning will find itself impotent in the face of a lack of market demand for development.

This chapter begins by reviewing the arguments made by economists for adopting a different benchmark for social progress to economic growth. It discusses the importance of tackling inequalities in the built environment, and incorporates these concerns within an environmental sustainability agenda using the concept of just sustainability. It then goes on to outline an agenda for planning practice that will frame the discussion of different approaches in the following three chapters. This is all brought together into a proposal for reform of the planning system in the final chapter of the book.

From growth to well-being

There is now a body of work that recognises that there are problems with the pursuit of economic growth as the main societal goal and indeed with GDP as the main measure of social and political success. Among the key proponents of this different way of thinking are Tim Jackson and Richard Layard.

Jackson's thesis, as set out in *Prosperity without growth*, develops from an analysis of the ecological limits placed on the scale of economic activity by the natural world within which we live, with a particular emphasis on resource scarcity and climate change, but also recognition of deforestation, biodiversity loss, soil degradation, collapse of fish stocks, water scarcity, pollution and contamination.[1] While he points out that 'Questioning growth is deemed to be the act of lunatics, idealists and revolutionaries' (p 14), he goes on to argue:

> But question it we must. The idea of a non-growing economy may be anathema to an economist. But the idea of a continually growing economy is anathema to an ecologist. No subsystem of a finite system can grow indefinitely, in physical terms. Economists have to be able to answer the question of how a continually growing economic system can fit within a finite ecological system. (p 14)

He makes the negative point that decoupling – delinking environmental impacts from the economic activity generating growth – has so far been very limited, and there is no prospect of it accelerating to achieve the scale of decoupling required to stay within ecological limits. Most policy measures emphasise relative decoupling, in which the ratio of environmental impact to GDP goes down. But if GDP continues to go up, this will still result in greater environmental burdens. Jackson argues that absolute decoupling is required in which environmental burdens go down in absolute terms and that conventional GDP-driven growth cannot achieve this.

As discussed in Chapter 5, the idea of green growth is seen as attractive as a way of creating a transition to a new type of economy, but Jackson criticises the logic of Keynesianism inherent in this approach, which looks to consumption growth and credit driving innovation, productivity and – once again – economic growth. 'A different way of ensuring stability and maintaining employment is needed' (p 119). So he makes the positive case, drawing on research from Canada, that it is possible to reduce economic growth (in this case from 1.8 per cent per annum to less than 0.1 per cent per annum) by manipulating the drivers of growth and to do so in a stable way that halves unemployment and poverty (p 135). In this modelling exercise, the ratio of debt to GDP is cut by 75 per cent and a 20 per cent reduction in greenhouse gases achieved.

Key elements within this transition are reduced working hours and a shorter working week in order to share out work more evenly across the population. Other elements include:

- Less focus on increasing labour productivity across the board, focusing instead on those areas where the work experience is poor, and ensuring that people have access to meaningful work experiences.
- A shift from consumption to investment at the level of the economy as a whole.
- Focused innovation addressing resource productivity, renewable energy, clean technology, green business, climate adaptation and ecosystem enhancement.

Jackson points out (p 130) that 'the seeds for such an economy may already exist in local or community-based social enterprises: community energy projects, local farmers' markets, slow food cooperatives, sports clubs, libraries, community health and fitness centres, local repair and maintenance services, craft workshops, writing centres, water sports, community music and drama, local training and skills. And yes, maybe even yoga (or martial arts or meditation), hairdressing and gardening.' He is pointing to 'a kind of Cinderella economy that sits neglected at the margins of consumer society' (p 131).

Layard's work takes a slightly different tack, focusing on the concept of happiness. He is seeking an approach that will deliver greater happiness within society. Partly this is a matter of recognising that ever-increasing income does not necessarily contribute to happiness. Layard has demonstrated this by collating data for individual countries and showing that, within a country over time, happiness is not connected to growth in income per head.[2] This is reinforced by the work of the Worldwatch Institute, who have analysed data on a cross-national basis and shown that after an income level of about US$15,000 per capita, the calculation for life satisfaction score hardly responds at all to further increases, even quite large increases, in national income.[3] Layard shows that poverty makes people unhappy relative to their wealthier compatriots, but becoming richer only makes one happier temporarily; the impact fades.[4]

Reconsidering the value of economic growth as a dominant goal also implies reconsidering how success with regard to societal goals is measured. Currently, we are reminded daily by the mass media and government of the need for economic growth, and the indicator *par excellence* of such growth is GDP and it slightly broader counterpart, gross national product (GNP). The reporting of GDP figures is a ritual that is almost sacrosanct in today's society. The announcement of new annual or quarterly figures usually merits a special news item, often breaking into other programmes (at the time of writing, Radio 5 was promising to break into live coverage of Andy Murray's semi-final tennis match at the Australian Open to 'bring you the latest GDP figures').

But the originator of GDP as an economic measure was less sure about its universal value. In 1962 Simon Kuznets warned that: 'The welfare of a nation can scarcely be inferred from a measurement of national income.'[5] A perhaps more famous indictment of GNP and what it measures is provided by a quote from a speech by Senator Robert F. Kennedy in March 1968:[6]

'We will find neither national purpose nor personal satisfaction in a mere continuation of economic progress, in an endless amassing of worldly goods. We cannot measure national spirit by the Dow Jones Average, nor national achievement by the Gross National Product....

It measures everything, in short, except that which makes
life worthwhile....'

The criticisms that have been targeted at GDP and GNP fall in two
main categories: what it measures and what it does not.

GDP is a measure of all goods and services that are produced,
consumed and – most importantly – exchanged within the market
system. Thus it includes a range of economic activities that are
associated with aspects of our society that would generally be
considered as undesirable: pollution, crime and addiction, for example.
In particular, resource depletion and the associated environmental
degradation are considered economic additions to GDP if they result
in items and services that are traded for money. No deductions are
made for adverse environmental impacts.

And GDP does not count anything that is not traded, even though
these elements may be essential for societal functioning, continued
economic activity and furthermore, contribute to our well-being.
Domestic services and childcare are paramount examples here.
Childcare by a childminder or in a nursery counts towards GDP;
that care provided by a parent or family member does not. This is not
to wade into an argument about how to nurture the development
of children; the point is rather that GDP draws a distinction simply
on the basis of economic trade. There is a whole range of untraded
activities that contribute to people's functioning and well-being,
including many social activities, from attending religious services
to being part of a choir or tending an allotment. None of these are
reflected in GDP calculations.

There are now a number of initiatives that seek to provide a new
metric to challenge the dominance of GDP. Most of these are aimed
at the national level and seek to influence central government policy.
But the discussions around this agenda have the potential to offer
a different view of what constitutes successful planning at the local
scale too.

An example that focuses particularly on incorporating a
concern with resource depletion and environmental degradation
is the Genuine Progress Index based on 26 social, economic and
environmental variables.[7] Attempts to identify a new measure of

economic wealth based on replacing the resource used in annual economic activity – termed the genuine savings or adjusted net savings rate – is another example of this approach.[8] The New Economics Foundation's exploration of National Accounts of Well-being and the Happy Planet Index are further examples.[9] Some countries, such as Norway, already produce Green National Income Accounts – alongside GDP – that incorporate these environmental concerns.[10]

In line with the happiness agenda, there have also been efforts to create measures more concerned with social well-being. Richard Layard has been particularly influential in getting the current Coalition government to develop a measure of national well-being.[11] The National Well-being Indicator Set currently covers three domains, as set out in Box 6.1.

Box 6.1: UK National Well-being Indicator Set
- Individual well-being
- Factors directly affecting individual well-being
  - Our relationships
  - Health
  - What we do
  - Where we live
  - Personal finance
  - Education and skills
- More contextual domains
  - Governance
  - The economy
  - The natural environment

The first set of well-being statistics was issued by the Office for National Statistics in July 2012. These identified the happiest locations (Orkney and Shetland, Rutland, Anglesey, Wiltshire and West Berkshire) as well at the least happy (North Ayrshire, Blaenau Gwent, Swansea, County Durham and Blackpool). It was clear that people living in built-up and former industrial areas were generally less happy than their more rural counterparts. But, as might be expected, good health, good relationships and some financial security also made people happier.

What this suggests is that a planning agenda that seeks to improve well-being would be a better basis for planning practice than one based on the promotion of local economic activity and market-led development alone. Of course, planners and politicians will claim that this is exactly what is currently being aimed at. However, the dominance of growth-dependent planning as a mode of delivery on policy goals clearly does not achieve this. Any such claims remain purely rhetorical devices.

Well-being, tackling inequalities and sustainability

It is also now being recognised that the scale of inequality within a country has detrimental effects on well-being. The reasons for this and even the data on this are not conclusively understood, but it can be hypothesised that happiness is related to how we see our situation in relation to others. Greater wealth and income disparities create more opportunities for seeing our situations as markedly inferior to someone else's. Furthermore, inequality is associated with a range of social problems such as crime and ill health, and these have a negative impact on people across society more generally. Research by Wilkinson and Pickett showed that people's well-being, as perceived subjectively and measured more objectively by a range of measures, increased with greater equality.[12] This suggests the importance of tackling social inequality within society, which Chapter 5 demonstrated is considerable within the UK.

Research led by Michael Marmot has looked in particular at the relationship between health, well-being and inequalities.[13] He investigated the links between socio-economic position and health at the international and nation scales, producing a 'social determinants of health' analysis. In the UK report *Fair society, healthy lives*, it is estimated that between 1.3 and 2.5 million extra years of life are lost as a result of people dying prematurely due to health inequalities.[14] Based on a wealth of evidence, this has demonstrated that 'people with a higher socioeconomic position in society have a greater array of life changes and more opportunities to lead a flourishing life. They also have better health' (p 3).

Using data at the neighbourhood scale, the research showed that life expectancy and also disability-free life expectancy rose as one moved from the most to the least deprived population percentiles. On average, people living in the poorest neighbourhoods die seven years earlier than those in the richest (p 10). The average difference in disability-free life expectancy is 17 years (this measures the average number of years that a person could expect to live without an illness or health problem that limits their daily activities). And this is not just a result of comparing extreme social positions; excluding the poorest and richest 5 per cent of the population still produces a difference in life expectancy of six years and disability-free life expectancy of 13 years. A two-year update in February 2012 looked at data for the 150 upper-tier local authorities due to take over responsibilities for public health under the Coalition government reforms. Comparing data for 2008–10 with 2007–09, this found that while life expectancy had increased for most of these areas, inequalities had also increased.

While the UK Marmot Review argued that reducing health inequalities would have economic benefits through greater labour productivity (£31–£33 billion per annum), larger tax revenue and reduced welfare payments (£20–£32 billion per annum) and lower treatment costs (in excess of £5.5 billion per annum), they also stated firmly: 'Economic growth is not the most important measure of our country's success. The fair distribution of health, well-being and sustainability are important social goals' (p 9).

The environmental justice literature addresses similar concerns. It has its origins in examining the spatial co-location of LULUs (locally unwanted land uses), such as waste sites, with disadvantaged communities, particularly communities of color in the US. Since then the environmental justice movement has broadened its remit in terms of considering a wider range of environmental impacts and of disadvantaged communities. It has also looked at environmental injustice not only in terms of the distribution of environmental goods and bads, but also considering the processes by which such communities are involved in decision-making and the recognition that is granted to such communities in terms of their specific identities and values. However, it is the distributional aspects that are of concern here.

In his excellent summary of the literature on environmental injustice, Walker provides a useful guide to the literature on the distribution of various environmental externalities in the UK context.[15] His review unpacks the difficulties of statistically demonstrating simple relationships of environmental injustice in terms of co-location of communities and LULUs, or the resultant distribution of health impacts. It can be summarised as follows:

- Waste sites: there seems to be co-location of low-income communities with recycling facilities and waste incineration plants but, because many landfill sites are in more rural locations, they are more often located nearer higher-income communities.
- Air quality: this often takes a U-shaped relationship with both the poorest and the wealthiest to be found living in locations with poor air quality, partly because of very high-income residents choosing to live in city centres. However, data on air quality is very difficult to use in such simple correlations because of limitations in monitoring practices and the mobility of air pollution and hence its impacts. Research focused on exceedences of air quality standards, however, seems to suggest a strong bias to breaches of standards in low-income areas.
- Flooding: there seems to be a strongly socially regressive gradient in exposure to flood risk, although this mainly applies to sea flooding. Such a pattern is much more difficult to detect in relation to river flooding. This is partly because higher-income groups often pay to locate in areas near rivers due to the positive externalities of riverside amenities.
- Urban green space: this is extremely difficult to research because the nature, amenity value and functionality of urban green space vary so much. Proximity also does not tell one much about the actual use of such spaces. Research on the latter suggests older people, minority ethnic groups, women and 12- to 19-year-olds are under-represented in green space use, but this does not map neatly onto socio-economic groupings.

It is often very complex to disentangle the different dimensions of environmental impact as they have an impact on different socio-economic groups. However, there does seem to be a case, at least, for paying attention to the potential adverse environmental impacts experienced by lower-income, disadvantaged and vulnerable groups within a local population.

Agyeman has made a strong case that the environmental justice agenda should be merged with the sustainability agenda.[16] This argument arises from concerns that the sustainability agenda tends to focus on common interests in a safe and well-functioning environment and doesn't fully acknowledge the different interests, values, cultures and socio-economic situations of different social groups in relation to the environment, both now and in the future. Agyeman develops a critique of the environmental sustainability agenda for prioritising climate protection, pollution control and environmental conservation over social concerns, and seeing such environmental policy action as necessarily to the benefit of all social groups. Instead he argues that environmental concerns should always be seen in relation to their impact on disadvantaged groups, and that they should be addressed in a way that takes full account of the identity, history and values of those groups.

He questions in particular whether ethnic diversity is sufficiently addressed in pursuing sustainability options in urban contexts, and argues for close attention to the needs, as culturally expressed, of such diverse groups. This is a strong argument for the benefits of community-based action that is able to take such a carefully nuanced approach. Such an approach is termed 'just sustainability'. Agyeman favours the plural – just sustainabilities – as recognising that there will be multiple interpretations and pathways towards more just and environmentally sustainable outcomes across localities and communities; however, for ease of expression, the singular is often deployed below.

Reframing planning for just sustainability

The above discussion has suggested that, instead of an overwhelming and unthinking adoption of growth dependence, planning policy and practice should adopt an approach that focuses on well-being, attention to inequalities and sustainability. Following Agyeman, a just sustainability frame is used to suggest a reformed planning agenda. Of course, planning on its own cannot deliver just sustainability. The Marmot Review pointed to the importance of household income, employment status, educational qualifications and the quality of early childcare in determining health inequalities. The kind of planning for urban change and improvement that the planning system can achieve, at its best, will not address all these aspects, and the arguments developed in the rest of this book are not intended as a substitute for making the case for a proper welfare system, that provides a nurturing environment for children from infancy onwards, lifelong education and adequate income support. These have to be part of the overall policy package. However, there are aspects of socio-spatial inequality and environmental sustainability that urban planning can readily help address, thereby promoting just sustainability.

Agyeman identifies four essential conditions for just and sustainable communities. The first of these is improvement in quality of life and well-being. The second is meeting the needs of both present and future generations, covering both intergenerational and intragenerational equity. Third, he looks to the importance of justice and equity in terms of recognition, processes, procedures and outcomes. And fourth and finally, he draws attention to the importance of living within ecosystem limits. This is a substantial and broad agenda. It looks to how planning is done and also what its outcomes are. There are many aspects of planning – urban, countryside, transport and environmental planning – that require reform to address this just sustainability agenda.

For example, and linking back to the origins of the environmental justice movement, issues of environmental risk are centrally implicated in just sustainability. Planning activity to reduce pollution levels and to reduce the exposure of communities to the risks posed by this and other environmental hazards is an important way of enhancing health and well-being. If there is an emphasis on the distribution of such hazards among social groups, and recognition of the need to protect lower-income groups from a disproportionate risk burden, then action for environmental justice can also be achieved.

While there is generally sufficient coverage of sewerage and water supply infrastructure across the UK to render the 19th-century public health concerns a matter of the past, there are still issues of water pollution to be addressed. Discharges to the sea continue to pollute a significant number of beaches, and there has been the need for substantial investment in a new holding sewer – the Thames Tideway Tunnel – under the Thames to prevent sewage overflows into the river during periods of heavy rainfall.[17] Turning to other media, land contamination is still a legacy of 19th-century industrialisation in certain locations. Despite considerable remediation work, this remains a problem. It has been estimated that in 2004 in England and Wales there were about 30,000 to 40,000 sites affected by land contamination, equating to 55,000 to 80,000 hectares.[18]

Other environmental risks that can have an impact on the well-being of households and, indeed, business owners, are associated with flooding and ground instability. Flooding can have a variety of causes including sea level rise, tidal surges, overflow of rivers due to excessive rainfall or snowmelt in catchment areas, and flash floods in urban areas due to rainfall accumulating on impervious surfaces. These risks are likely to be exacerbated in the future by heavier rainfall periods due to climate change. Ground instability in the UK is largely associated with the long-lived results of mining where past excavations can undermine the stability of buildings.[19] However, coastal erosion also has a role to play, and will also be affected by climate change and associated sea level rise. Climate change will further create ground instability in clay soil areas during periods of low rainfall, when such soils shrink.[20] These risks are often discussed in terms of the economic costs that result and, in particular, the costs to the insurance industry. However, for more vulnerable households the costs are, first, the stress associated with dealing with an episode of flooding or subsidence and, second, the financial costs for households and businesses unwilling or unable to pay for insurance.

Another important area to tackle for just sustainability concerns mobility. Moving around urban environments is essential if people are to benefit from the facilities on offer for employment, consumption, education, leisure and other services and to fulfil the vital need to meet other people. Some of these movements are more local, others more distant. Spatial planning can seek to plan land uses so that more of these requirements for mobility relate to shorter rather than longer distances, and there has been a strong movement towards encouraging more dense urban settlements as a means of enhancing the proximity of different land uses to one another and reducing distance travelled. This is seen as a major contribution to mitigating greenhouse gas emissions.[21] However, this only offers the potential for shorter journeys; it does not ensure them. People may choose to use a facility further afield, or have to travel further for work reasons.

Travel in itself need not be harmful to individual well-being. However, there are significant impacts on others of road-based travel. Leaving aside the financial costs (personal and commercial) of congestion, there are the health impacts of the diffuse air pollution that motor vehicles generate, together with the noise. Concern with climate change emphasises the emissions that generate carbon dioxide; while the absolute total of greenhouse gases associated with transport has stayed broadly unchanged over 1990–2009, transport emissions as a share of all domestic greenhouse gas emissions have risen from 16 to 22 per cent.[22] Turning to other emissions to air, road-based transport is implicated in a range of pollutants: particulates, carbon monoxide, nitrogen oxide and benzene.[23] In London, traffic is responsible for 99 per cent of carbon monoxide, 76 per cent of nitrogen oxide and 90 per cent of hydrocarbons. Translated into health impacts, this pollution is estimated to be responsible for between 12,000 and 24,000 premature deaths, and a further 14,000 to 24,000 hospital admissions.

Another negative health impact associated with road transport is accidents. In the UK, 2,605 people died in 2009 in road traffic accidents, with 25 per cent of all deaths for 15- to 19-year-olds due to such accidents.[24] Then there is the impact of the use of cars in creating a sedentary lifestyle and the impact that this has on physical weight and health. The Government Office for Science Foresight report on *Tackling obesities* reported that obesity rates had doubled in the last 25 years, with a quarter of adults and 10 per cent of children being obese, and 20–25 per cent of children being overweight; it was anticipated that 40 per cent of Britons would be obese by 2025.[25] In addition, there are issues over access to and the cost of such car-based travel, and equity concerns regarding social groups reliant on public transport or walking because of such costs.

Although acknowledging that these environmental risks and aspects of mobility are important to address for just sustainability, the focus here is rather on areas of urban planning policy and practice more closely connected to the growth-dependent paradigm. In particular, subsequent chapters address the way that areas, particularly low-income areas, can be supported through different forms of urban development, area enhancement and community asset management. They will examine the role that the urban planning system can play in supporting low-income communities, protecting their areas, services and facilities, and working towards improved local quality of life while also having regard to broader environmental sustainability concerns. The issues that are particularly relevant here concern the contribution to equality and sustainability that can be made through improved housing standards, availability and affordability, and through improving the broader public realm, including the green public realm. The importance of these two aspects will be briefly reviewed.

Dealing with housing inadequacies and shortages

The existence of inadequate housing was one of the prime drivers for the 19th-century legislation that lies at the roots of the modern planning system. Such housing was typified by overcrowding, pest infestation, damp and a lack of ventilation. It came to be known by the highly pejorative term, 'slum', thus justifying extensive slum clearance in the early-mid 20th century. While the worst of such slum-like conditions have been eradicated, people still live in housing which is overcrowded, damp and unsuitable for habitation. In addition, the experience of sheer homelessness is still with us. The statistics on housing availability and conditions point to a number of severe problems[26] (the following figures are all for England alone).

It is clear that there is an absolute shortage of housing available at costs that households can afford. There were 1.85 million households on council housing waiting lists in 2012, almost 70,000 children in temporary accommodation in the third quarter of 2012, and 13,566 households were accepted as homeless by local authorities in the fourth quarter of 2012. Completion rates for new housing are low, with 105,590 dwellings completed in 2011/12, of which 58,000 counted as 'affordable' but only just over 24,000 were housing association dwellings and less than 2,000 were local authority dwellings. Factoring in demographic change, it is estimated that new build rates need to be over double this to meet demand.[27] But costs of housing also have to be addressed if housing need, as opposed to aggregate demand, is to be met. Just to give an indication of the rental gap that exists between the social and private sectors: in the first quarter of 2012, private sector rents (on a rolling one-year basis) ranged from £468 per week in the North East to £1,312 in London; the average rents in the housing association sector for 2011 were £65.78 and £97.46 respectively and for council housing in 2011/12 they were £59.38 and £89.17 respectively.

The standard of housing also needs to be addressed. Damp and poor indoor air quality lead to mould formation with consequent health impacts; the 2010 English Housing Survey found that 7 per cent of dwellings had damp problems.[28] Housing does not always provide sufficient thermal comfort. Fuel poverty refers to the situation where a household has to spend over 10 per cent of their income on heating; the statistics on the number of households in fuel poverty vary with the price of energy, but in 2010 it was estimated that this described 3.5 million households in England and 4.75 million in the UK.[29] In addition, the changing climate may mean that many houses provide inadequate ventilation and cooling during heat waves. Past episodes of extremely high temperatures sustained over several weeks have seen a spike in mortality rates, particularly among older people.[30]

The solution to these problems lies in new housing development and the upgrading or replacement of inadequate housing to provide proper shelter from the external environment, but doing so in a way that enables lower-income households to gain access to decent accommodation and reduces the carbon emissions associated with domestic energy use.

The benefits of an improved public realm

People do not just live in their homes. The public realm is essential for carrying out everyday activities, accessing livelihoods, pursuing personal enjoyment and developing social contacts. It provides the setting for the range of services and facilities that people need: shopping, leisure possibilities, education, healthcare, and so on. It also provides the setting for employment opportunities. The public realm knits together all the elements of urban living and thus the quality of that public realm, and the way that it supports local communities is an essential element of just sustainability. While this includes many buildings for different land uses – employment, services – it also involves the open spaces between such buildings. The quality and nature of these open spaces has a considerable impact on well-being for different social groups. If adequate housing is probably the first requirement of planning for justice and sustainability, then a quality public realm comes a close second.[31]

There are a number of different dimensions of this but, in particular, it is widely accepted that the physical features of the public realm contribute to mental and physical health. Green infrastructure seems to be an important dimension of this. Such greenery has been shown to contribute to mental states of well-being and to act as an aid to the recovery of health.[32] For example, for workers, spending time in green spaces planted with trees reduces stress and mental fatigue and can enhance productivity and creativity. The symptoms of a variety of conditions such as Alzheimer's, dementia and depression are alleviated by outdoor activity. These are in addition to the potential of green spaces to offer opportunities for physical activity and active mobility that can increase physical fitness and reduce obesity. The provision of outdoor spaces that are attractive and safe are likely to encourage such outdoor activity with health benefits arising from reduced obesity levels and improved cardio-vascular condition, and also environmental benefits in terms of reduced carbon emissions.

This is important for all age groups, but the provision of areas for outdoor play for children may be particularly important in avoiding problems of being over-weight and unfit at a later stage, and establishing patterns of active mobility. A research review undertaken by the RSPB has argued strongly for the benefits of outdoor play by children in terms of education, mental and physical health and also developing personal and social skills.[33] Looking particularly at the benefits of such contact with nature for children with Attention Deficit Hyperactivity Disorder (ADHD), this found that: 'Outdoor activities in nature appear to improve symptoms of ADHD in children by 30% compared with urban outdoor activities and threefold compared with the indoor environment.' This was reinforced by a review conducted by the University of Washington, which found benefits in terms of cognitive, emotional, intellectual, imaginative and behavioural development for children in having contact with nature.[34]

Green areas can also reduce air pollution if appropriate planting is provided.[35] Furthermore, natural vegetation can act as a noise buffer; water features can also cloak noise. Green and blue infrastructure (that is, various water features) are likely to be more significant in the future with climate change as they can help reduce the impact of heat stress during extended periods of high temperatures,[36] of particular relevance to London and the South East of the UK under climate change.

There has been a recent emphasis on the potential for the outdoor environment to provide a space for urban or suburban horticulture.[37] This has a number of benefits. It involves physical activity and thus acts as a form of exercise. It also provides a source of food and, most importantly, a source of fresh fruit and vegetables. These can help meet baseline nutritional needs, and also are exactly the kinds of food that contribute to a healthy diet. In situations where access to cheap fruit and vegetables is difficult because of the local structure of retailing, these additions to the household diet can be important for health and family budgeting.

The need for reformed planning institutions

Achieving just sustainability requires a different approach to the growth-dependent planning that has dominated in the past. New institutions of planning are needed with different planning tools and modes of operation. Such planning institutions can be analysed in terms of three elements: the objectives as framed by the policy agenda and reflecting the embedded values of the organisations involved; the processes that these organisations engage in and which provide the institutional dynamics; and the specific delivery tools that are available so that the institutional dynamics are able to meet the institutional objectives.

Figure 6.1 sets this framework out in simple diagrammatic form. It supplies a version of the framework for the paradigm of growth-dependent planning (Figure 6.1a) that outlines the objectives as set by market values supplemented by the desire for social and environmental side-benefits. The processes are described as a form of skewed collaboration with limited public participation, and the delivery tools comprise indicative plans combined with regulation and associated negotiation. As has been discussed, growth-dependent planning can be more effective if regulation within the planning system is strong enough and negotiation by planners effective enough, together with an underlying community acceptance of the

Figure 6.1a: Institutional framework of growth-dependent planning

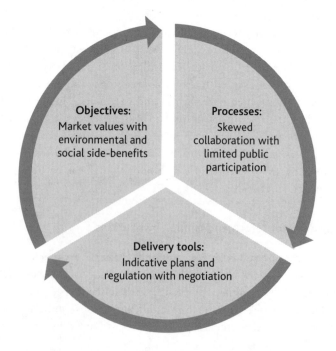

development that the market has proposed and the planning gain that can be negotiated. These conditions do not always apply, however.

In Figure 6.1b the outlines of an alternative approach are set out. In line with the discussion in this chapter, the objectives would be framed in terms of well-being, tackling inequalities and sustainability, that is, just sustainability. This will be quite challenging. It should be recognised that the UK planning system has tended to shy away from identifying action focused on specific social groups, the only exception probably being provision for those with a physical disability. Instead, planning policy has sought to promote change to the built environment that can be argued to benefit substantial sections of society (such as an improved urban realm) or undefined groups within society (such as those seeking access to adequate housing). It has not argued for or enabled action to favour a specific income group or housing tenure, for example. This fundamental issue is returned to in Chapters 7 to 9.

Figure 6.1b: Institutional reforms for planning beyond growth dependence

Objectives:
Well-being, tackling
inequalities and
sustainability =
just sustainability

Processes:
A new role for
planners and different
forms of community
engagement

Delivery tools:
An expanded toolkit

The reforms would also imply a new role for planners and different forms of community engagement. And an expanded planning toolkit would be needed. The description of the institutional arrangements for planning beyond growth dependence is necessarily sketchy at this stage in the book. The following chapters explore a variety of ways that the planning system can adopt new tools and means to implement the just sustainability agenda and, until this exploration has been undertaken, it is not possible to provide more detail. By Chapter 10 a fuller account can be given of how the institutions of the planning system should be changed to deliver on the reformed planning agenda set out here.

SEVEN

Alternative development models

In this chapter the focus is on alternative models of urban development to the growth-dependent approach, having particular regard to how diverse social needs can be met through such development, including the needs of lower-income households and the provision of affordable housing for such households. The term 'affordable' here is not used in any technical sense or limited by current policy terminology; it is just used to emphasise the importance of providing housing that lower-income households are able to afford. While this chapter begins with such considerations of affordability in relation to housing, the development models considered also provide the potential for a broader understanding of how to meet community needs, including some environmental sustainability concerns.

Affordable housing

The limitations of growth-dependent planning

The core problem where affordability is concerned is that market processes are oriented towards generating new development that meets the demands of those with purchasing power.[1] This does not mean that all development has to be aimed at the highest value end of the market, those with the most purchasing power. As described in Chapter 3, much depends on the balance between the demand for new property in the market and all the costs of providing that development, including materials, professional fees and labour, and also land and finance. This can mean that the gap between development prices and costs of provision are such that medium- rather than high-priced development is what the market actors perceive as the appropriate niche to try and fill in a specific location at a particular time. However, markets tend not to deliver the lowest value property, at least in terms of new development, leaving it to adjustments in the existing stock to meet this demand, often through dilapidated or space-constrained properties. A greater profit can usually be made by building higher value developments.

Previous chapters have shown how growth-dependent planning uses the tools of planning gain and leverage to provide for community needs. Under the New Labour government, it was used to require that a share of a housing development was provided as affordable housing.[2] In London, this proportion rose to as high as 50 per cent under Ken Livingstone's Mayoral regime at the Greater London Authority. This substantial percentage was rendered feasible by the high demand for housing in the city combined with another policy of the time, increasing the permitted density of development. In these circumstances, residential development was very profitable and there was considerable potential to negotiate successfully for a substantial provision of affordable housing within new developments. Current government policy has moved away from strong requirements for affordable housing. Under proposals currently being put forward by the Montague Commission, requirements to provide affordable housing are likely to be dropped, at least where building for rent is concerned,[3] and in terms of housing for sale, the emphasis has shifted towards assessing whether currently agreed levels of affordable housing are threatening the viability of development sites.[4]

The other strategy that growth-dependent planning has available is to subsidise new development so that lower-priced development can be built at profit. As discussed in Chapter 3, this can be through subsidies to the development, as with urban regeneration grants over the decades. The subsidy can also be hidden in a lower land value, with the state taking the role of providing cheaper land to developers. This was the dynamic behind the redevelopment of the London Docklands, for example, where huge areas of land were transferred by a simplified procedure into the ownership of the London Docklands Development Corporation and then passed on to developers at prices that made housebuilding and other development profitable. The Montague Commission is currently proposing that publicly owned land is 'lent' to developers (including housing associations) building for rent, with repayment on eventual sale to a long-term landlord.

However, while both these strategies can be effective in circumstances where there is a relatively buoyant market demand, they are less so when market demand falls. Negotiated public benefits will become harder to achieve as developers argue – possibly quite plausibly – that they cannot afford them, and subsidies may, at best, just get the development to go ahead rather than support the provision of substantial social benefits. In the past, the solutions to this problem have either promoted deregulation or relied on state provision.

Tackling housing affordability through deregulation within the planning system

There is an argument that is regularly propounded in planning debates that planning regulation itself is the reason that lower-value developments are not built. Proponents of this view see regulation as restricting the overall supply of new development and thereby driving up its price. This argument is particularly applied to the housing market to explain the lack of housing for local needs or new entrants to the market. Here the tendency of the planning system to 'contain' urban development, to use Peter Hall's famous description, is emphasised.[5] Such containment arises from two sources. On the one hand there is the mix of specific designations such as green belts, National Parks, Areas of Outstanding Natural Beauty and Conservation Areas, which are intended to restrict new development. These have combined with the ability of some residents to influence development control processes so that new development proposals are resisted, so-called NIMBYism.

Together these reasons can be considered part of the explanation for the declining housebuilding rates over the last half-century, as illustrated in Figure 7.1. This shows a peak in 1954 and then a further higher peak in 1968. Since then completions fell to below 200,000 in 1982 and stayed at around that figure until the recent economic crisis, with a huge decline from just over 226,000 dwellings completed in 2007 down to less than 139,000 in 2010.

Figure 7.1: Housebuilding: completions, 1949–2010

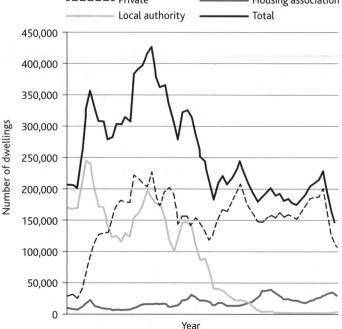

Source: Data from tables at www.gov.uk/government/statistical-data-sets/
live-tables-on-house-building

The net effect of reduced supply, it is argued, is a higher level of prices for new developments, and housing prices have indeed risen significantly, as Figure 7.2 shows. This provides an index of house prices, adjusted for the mix of different types of housing in different years. There was a dip in 1989 to 1993 and then around 2008–09, but otherwise the national average for prices of all houses (new and existing) has risen. Prices for new housing follow the same trend, with a price discount for new housing of up to 6 per cent. This discount increased to almost 10 per cent in the crisis of the early 1970s and again in the recent economic turmoil.

The answer would, therefore, seem to be relaxation of planning regulation to allow more development to occur, thus driving house prices down through increased supply. This was the policy advocated

Figure 7.2: House price index, 1969–2010

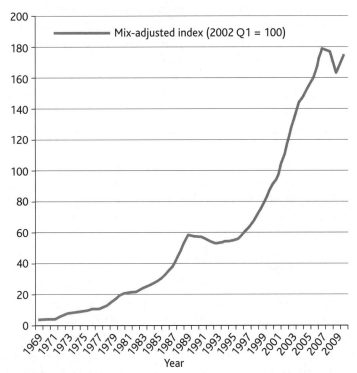

Source: Data from tables at www.gov.uk/government/statistical-data-sets/
live-tables-on-housing-market-and-house-prices

in the influential Barker Review[6] in the 1990s, and also by the
Conservative Thatcher government in the 1980s and the Coalition
government currently. However, this is not a full analysis of the
problem as is clear when private sector completions are considered
alongside the house price index. There are other supply-side factors,
such as the costs of housebuilding and the role of landownership by
housebuilders, and there are also demand-side factors.

The UK housebuilding industry is not known for investment in
modern production methods that would reduce costs, for example,
through economies of scale and the application of new technologies.
Housebuilding remains a rather traditional industry, certainly
as compared with many European countries. The ability of the

housebuilding industry to make profits from restricted as well as expansive levels of development should also not be discounted. As well as profiting from the sale and hence development of each dwelling – which obviously would favour more rather than less development – housebuilders also favour market circumstances that maintain the price level for their new housing, and thus have an interest in a degree of restricted supply, or rather, perhaps, a managed supply. Insofar as housebuilders own landbanks, they also have an interest in planning policies that keep the value of those landbanks high. Again, unrestricted supply may not be favoured as this will devalue those landbanks. Rather, a managed release of land, in particular land in their landbanks, will be the favoured approach.[7]

The impact of demand–side factors on house prices is tied up with mortgage finance. Given that housing is an expensive good that most people cannot pay out for out of their disposable income, house purchase is dependent on debt, on obtaining a mortgage. This means that the availability and cost of mortgages will be a major influence on house prices. This is illustrated in Figure 7.3, which shows how the ratio of price to income follows a very similar pattern to the ratio for advances to income. It could be argued that this just reflects the needs of borrowers; as house prices go up, they need to borrow more. But this is a private market, and the point is that they would not be able to buy without the credit offered through mortgages; sellers, including developers, can achieve higher prices because higher loans are available.

The complications in the links between the supply of more affordable new housing, the supply of housing more generally and the role of planning in permitting more new development mean that deregulation is unlikely to be a very effective policy. Supply would have to increase very substantially indeed to offset the high demand pressures and to bring prices down. In addition, the housing market, in common with other property markets, seems to be 'downwardly sticky' so that prices rise more easily than they fall. Homeowners, when faced with potentially falling house prices, often take their property off the market rather than sell at a lower price. Thus the supply of existing houses tends to dry up during price downturns; only those who really need to or are wishing to downsize will sell.

Figure 7.3: Ratios of house prices and mortgages to income, 1969–2010

Source: Data from tables at www.gov.uk/government/statistical-data-sets/
live-tables-on-housing-market-and-house-prices

Since house prices are influenced by the total supply of housing in an area – new build and also turnover in the existing stock – this will slow any falls in house prices due to planning deregulation. Furthermore, landowning housebuilders may also seek to wait out falls in house prices rather than see the value of their landbanks fall. Or they may manage the supply of new housing in a locality through drip-feeding development in smaller amounts so as not to flood the market and undermine their own profits through an over-supply.

Finally, it should be remembered that the restrictive policies of the planning system also have purposes in terms of countryside protection and spatial land management. If deregulation was really to be pursued with sufficient enthusiasm to drive house prices down, this might well undermine these other important purposes of planning regulation that have considerable public and political support.

There is also a strong argument that the protection of the affordability of housing does not really lie within the remit of the planning system which is oriented towards shaping and regulating new development and urban change; rather, this is a matter of housing policy. In particular it is a matter of offering affordable housing outside the influence of marketplace dynamics and controlling the affordability of housing that is provided through such market dynamics. This latter element has, in the past, taken the form of controls on the cost of housing in the private sector. This has not applied to the cost of owner-occupied housing but rather to the rents that can be charged by private sector landlords. Although not currently an active element of housing policy, rent control has been used from time to time to limit how much a private landlord may charge; social landlords (that is, housing associations) are still subject to constraints on final rents as a condition of their funding grants.[8]

However, such rent control has been severely criticised for the negative impacts it has on the supply of rented property. Since such property is being supplied by the market, supply will respond to the profitability of investment in rented housing compared to other investment opportunities. Clearly rent control limits such profits and, therefore, it has tended to go with a reduction in the availability of properties to rent. The security of tenancy that is a key element of rent control – otherwise a landlord can replace the sitting tenant with another one who will be willing to pay more – also leads to rigidity in supply. Tenants do not move even when they may wish to for family or employment reasons because they fear they will not be able to get another home at an equivalent rent. In the face of such criticisms, rent control for the private sector was progressively deregulated in the latter 20th century. Private sector rents now largely find a level determined by market supply and demand. This clearly puts some households under severe financial stress, unable to gather enough capital to even consider home purchase, but faced with rents that are a considerable proportion of weekly income.

In cases where housing costs push families into the safety net of the welfare system, the policy response has been to cover at least some of the rent through housing benefit. This is a very expensive approach, however, and one that only further inflates private sector rents by subsidising demand. Much of the housing benefit goes straight through to landlords in the form of higher rents. Hence, in conditions of public sector retrenchment, payments for housing benefit are being reduced through a number of measures: a penalty for under-occupation (the so-called 'bedroom tax'); a cap on eligible rents according to property size; a linking of eligible rents to the 30th percentile of local market rents (rather than, as previously, the median); and a cap on the maximum benefit that a household can receive.[9] This is resulting in pressure for households to move out of more expensive rental markets to lower-value areas.

From this brief discussion, it should be clear that the main way to provide affordable housing is to develop a housing policy that offers low-cost rental housing outside of the marketplace. There is little substitute for public sector housing offered at low rents.

Public sector development: the historic option

Given these limitations in market-led approaches to meeting housing needs, there have been periods when direct state provision of housing was the route taken. A closer look at Figure 7.1 shows the importance of council housing within total housing completions, at least until 1976. In 1954 local authority-built housing accounted for 68 per cent of all completions; in 1968 it was 43 per cent of completions. But since 1976 it has declined down to a mere few hundreds per annum being built. This trend was slightly bucked in 2010 with an increase, but only to 1,360 dwellings completed. What lay behind this massive decline in local authority housing?

One can point to a mix of intense dissatisfaction with the quality of public sector housing that was built, particularly high-rise housing, and investment in new technologies that turned out to be unsafe. There were routine problems of damp, mould and inadequate heating systems. The design of estates failed to provide good quality and safe play areas for children, and instead produced a lack of 'defensible space', argued by some to be responsible for a rise in anti-social and even criminal behaviour on such estates. Then there was the notorious

Ronan Point disaster in East London when a gas explosion in one flat led to the collapse of several floors of a tower block. This came to stand for the inadequacy of council housing.

However, the nail in the coffin of local authority housing came with the ideologically driven policies of the Conservative government from 1979 onwards. This introduced the Right to Buy policy under which council tenants were able to buy their existing homes at a considerable discount. The idea was to give such households a share of the increases in the value of housing that owner-occupiers had enjoyed and, more generally, to give them a stake in a society based on equity ownership. The initial operation of the Right to Buy meant that it was no longer viable for local authorities to build homes as they could very swiftly be sold at a discount to the cost of building them. There was also for a time a dispute over how the receipts from council house sales could be spent. The current policy is that receipts should be used to provide an affordable home on a one-for-one replacement basis.[10]

The aim was that the residual need for social housing would be taken up by the housing association sector but, as Figure 7.1 shows, they have never contributed above 39,000 completions (that figure in 1995). Housing associations operate largely like private developers in terms of new development, but have the benefit of a substantial government subsidy to both their development and management activities. As a result they are able to offer housing to rent at a level below market rents. However, there are concerns over whether housing associations can actually provide sufficient affordable housing, particularly in high-rent areas. The current National Affordable Rent Programme provides a subsidy to housing association development, but cuts in the housing budget of 60 per cent through the Comprehensive Spending Review have resulted in the subsidy being spread more thinly over the targeted number of homes, so that near market (up to 80 per cent) rents are being charged in new social lets and a percentage of re-lets. Housing associations are expected to run down their balance sheets to provide greater affordability. The Joseph Rowntree Foundation argues that, as a result, in some areas social housing rents are at or even above market rents.[11]

Housing associations also offer a range of shared ownership options, whereby households are able to pay an amount every week or month that partly covers the rent and partly goes towards the purchase of some equity in their home. But these arrangements may not be any more affordable. A housing association development in Islington, London is reported as providing 60 shared ownership, affordable flats through a government grant of £20 million, but the buyers would need an income of double the London average to be able to buy a 25 per cent share in the largest flats and an income of around the London average to buy this share in the smaller ones.[12]

A further problem with any such schemes is that they transfer housing from being a service (providing housing) whose cost (rent) can be controlled by the social landlord to an asset (housing equity) whose price is determined by market fluctuations. While buyers under shared ownership may potentially benefit from rises in house prices, they also run the risks associated with a market downturn whereby the value of their equity share may actually fall below the value of the mortgage that was taken out to buy it, that is, falling into negative equity.

If a household does benefit from an increase in house prices and decides to sell on the market to realise that increase, this particular household is in a better situation, but the property is removed from being part of the ongoing supply of affordable housing. It is impossible to control the price of equity in housing after the first sale. Even in countries where public landownership is effective in producing low-cost housing for sale, such as Sweden and Germany, this can cause problems in the long term. Only in countries with a communist past, such as Belarus (in the former Soviet Union), is the price at which housing is sold controlled.

The housing association sector clearly plays an important role in providing social housing. However, within a growth-dependent model this can only be a limited role and it remains dependent on, first, government subsidy and, second, market demand making negotiation for such social housing a viable possibility. The question is whether there are other models of development that can allow housing associations to play a larger role and, more generally, provide a means for meeting diverse social needs through urban change. The rest of this chapter considers such models.

The Garden City model

For many, the Garden Cities remain the epitome of what planning can achieve: a designed environment that balances a variety of needs and pressures. In particular they are lauded for balancing town and country, maximising the benefits of both locations and avoiding the worst problems of both. The famous three magnets diagram captured this in pictorial form. As visually important was the social city diagram that suggested an elegant spatial layout for a cluster of developments organised around a functioning public transport system. Thus the Town and Country Planning Association (TCPA), the guardians of the Garden City ideal, identify the Garden City vision as combining:[13]

> ... the very best of town and country living to create healthy homes for working people in vibrant communities. The heart of the garden city ideals are holistically planned new settlements which enhance the natural environment, provide high quality affordable housing and locally accessible jobs.

However, the real innovation in the Garden City model lay not in its notions of urban design, spatial planning or transport infrastructure. Rather it was the financial model at the heart of Ebenezer Howard's *To-morrow: A peaceful path to real reform* (1898) that was really innovative. Although the TCPA put 'Community ownership of land and long term stewardship of assets' as the first among the key principles of Garden Cities, this aspect has been much less copied than the other elements.[14]

The essence of the financial model was the retention of the freehold of all land in the Garden City development area by a trust. All development rights were then granted on the basis of long leaseholds. This then provided a stream of income into the Garden City trust as freeholder through the ground rents paid by the leaseholders. It

Figure 7.4: The Garden City model

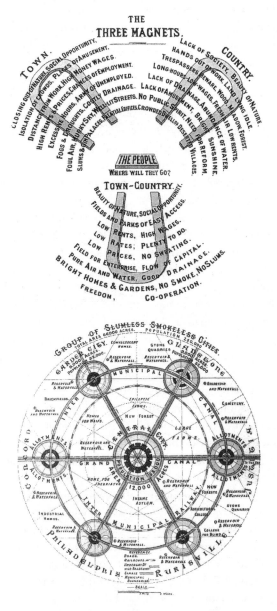

also meant that the value of the land was vested in the trust and they were able to benefit from increases in land values.

A good example of this is provided by Letchworth, the first Garden City to be developed in the UK.[15] Started in 1903, the First Garden City Ltd began with 3,818 acres of land in Hertfordshire. It boasts the UK's first roundabout and first purpose-built cinema. In 1962, the assets, role and responsibilities of this company were transferred to Letchworth Garden City Corporation and then, in 1995, to Letchworth Garden City Heritage Foundation. By this time the estate was worth £56 million. It now yields £2.6 million each year in rents from shops, offices and industrial space, and covers 5,500 acres, housing 33,600 people. Half of the housing in Letchworth is classified as social or affordable housing.

The ownership of the estate by the Foundation means that there is an ongoing source of income to meet local needs in a framework that is not wholly dependent on attracting further private sector investment to provide social benefits. In 2011, the Foundation had over £3 million available to invest back into the town through charitable activities and grants. Among the services provided are: the Broadway Cinema, the Community Hub, the Day Hospital, the Greenway (13.6 mile path around the town), the First Garden City Heritage Museum, a minibus service, Shopmobility service, Standalone Farm and the Tourist Information Centre. In addition, funds go to improvements in the landscaping of the town.

The Foundation structure also provides a mechanism for ongoing engagement with local communities. Indeed, 'dedication to open communication' is one of the four key principles of the Foundation, alongside a commitment to sustainability, a positive, pioneering approach and recognition of Letchworth's significance as the world's first Garden City. This means that the Foundation consulted early on about the Letchworth Garden City Town Centre Strategy, a document that the North Hertfordshire District Council then took forward to formal adoption in 2007. Thus landownership for the collective community benefit goes alongside community engagement, both driving the planning of the local area.

A similar model, in some ways, can be found in the great landed estates such as those owning and managing the central London areas of Belgravia and Mayfair. The similarity is the use of the freehold and long leasehold model to both retain control over and derive financial benefit from development and growth in the area. The difference, however, is that the Garden City model is clearly established for the communal benefit of the local residents and businesses, whereas in the great estates model the benefits accrue to the private landowner, and the ownership and management vehicle – the estates body – may have private rather than public interests at heart.

So what this discussion emphasises is the difference it makes to the planning of a locality if landownership is vested in the community through an appropriate institutional mechanism. This provides a degree of insulation from the influence of market forces so that benefits for the community can be more readily extracted through the role of landowner rather than planning regulator and negotiator. Many of the much-vaunted examples of good planning overseas are based in such landownership by the local planning authority.[16] For example, in Freiburg, Germany, and Stockholm, Sweden, the local authority ensures ownership of the land it plans for development, leading to exciting model developments such as Vaubun in Freiburg and Hammerby Sjöstad in Stockholm. This has been the opposite of the approach adopted for the last 50 years in the UK where bodies such as development corporations have been used to pass land directly to developers at a subsidised price rather than as a means of retaining freehold landownership for short-term control and long-term financial benefit.

In a 2012 report, the TCPA explored the potential for the Garden City model to be relevant today.[17] At the outset it established the importance of 'unlocking land': 'The Garden City vision cannot be realised without access to the right land in the right place at the right price.' By this it meant the provision of land from the public estate. It foresaw a role for government in assembling and releasing – in a coordinated way – public sector land, and asked for the reconsideration of the rules concerning the need to achieve 'best value' on public sector land sales, rules that buy into the growth-dependent approach and require development to be at the highest market value, through developers' bids for the land maximising the prices paid. Instead, the TCPA argued that a case should be made for sale at below market value to enable the desired development to go ahead.

The other element that they emphasised was infrastructure investment to 'de-risk' development for investors. Again this amounts to a subsidy to private sector development (see Chapter 3). They argued that local authorities should be able to borrow against expected income from the CIL to fund such infrastructure or even from the New Homes Bonus (see Chapter 3). The whole approach of this document is for local authorities and developers to share 'risk and reward'. But this is effectively cementing the local authority into a market-led and growth-dependent model. This is likely to be effective only in places where there is market demand for development, or where a marginally unviable development can be turned into a viable one through a combination of public sector-supported infrastructure investment and subsidised land transfers. This does not amount to the modern-day use of the original financial model at the heart of the Garden City movement, which would require community retention of all land ownership in the form of freeholds.

Community development and land trusts

New mechanisms have also arisen that vest ownership more directly in local communities and enable them to exercise control and build a stewardship role. This section explores such innovative mechanisms.

Operating under a variety of names – amenity trust, environment trust, community development company – a development trust is a form of partnership organisation that can undertake a variety of activities to benefit the local community. For example, they may:

- develop land with SME workspaces, sports and recreation facilities or low-cost housing;
- regenerate and refurbish buildings, open spaces and the public realm;
- manage and run workspaces, shops, market areas, public open spaces, community facilities and childcare centres; and
- offer training, education and advice services and engage in community development.

Being financially self-sufficient and not dependent on grants is central to their business model. They can build up a land or property base that then earns them income, in the model of the early Garden Cities. The aim is to create assets in the locality and to build up the value of those assets over time, with any profit being ploughed back into the community. The most frequent structure is a company limited by guarantee, which has members as opposed to shareholders, and reinvests rather than distributes any surplus. Charitable status can bring tax advantages but also limits some trading activities, requiring a subsidiary trading company to be set up that then covenants profits back to the parent charitable company.

Community land trusts (CLTs) are legally defined in the 2008 Housing and Regeneration Act, Section 79. A CLT is a mechanism for holding land in the long term for the benefit of the community. It works by separating out the value of the building(s) from the land that the building(s) stand on, with the community owning the latter outright. This enables the building(s) – which may include housing and/or other community assets – to be run at permanently affordable costs. Management of the CLT is community-based, often involving considerable volunteer time and effort. A number of different legal forms may be used, but they are often constituted as an Industrial and Provident Society or a company limited by guarantee. Sometimes they have charitable status, but this is not essential to their nature. They are, however, locally driven, locally controlled and locally accountable.

There is a CLT Fund that provides finance for feasibility studies, technical assistance and capital loans to supplement secured commercial development financing.[18] In addition, local authorities may offer support and parish council precepts (their share in council tax receipts) can be used, particularly for the pre-development phase. Local authorities are also empowered to finance development through, for example, a capital grant, revolving loan or deferred interest payment arrangement. Funding may also come from the Homes and Communities Agency, and CLTs sometimes partner with housing associations to develop residential schemes. Indeed the majority of CLTs are focused on providing affordable housing.[19] But as Table 7.1 shows, they have also been used to promote other forms of community-oriented development and activity that require landownership to be effective.

An early example of a development trust and CLT is provided by the Coin Street Community Builders (CSCB), that transformed 13 acres of derelict land on the south bank of the Thames into a thriving mixed-use neighbourhood.[20] It was set up in 1984 by local residents who had formed the Coin Street Action Group, and was

Table 7.1: Non-housing activities of community land trusts (CLTs)

Name	Location	Status	Non-housing element	Additional housing?
Bootle CLT	Cumbria	Not yet formally constituted	Tourism and energy	Yes
Brampton and Beyond Development Trust	Cumbria	Formally constituted, working up scheme	Extra care and environmental schemes	Yes
Cym Harry	Central Wales	Not yet formally constituted	Local food production and food recycling	No
Foundation East, Halesworth	Suffolk	Completed	Workspaces, community shop, community meeting room	Yes
High Bickington Community Property Trust	Devon	Under development	Workspaces	Yes
Lands End Peninsula CLT	Cornwall	Significant progress working up scheme	Community farm	No
North Kilworth	Leicestershire	Formally constituted, working up scheme	Energy and decarbonising schemes	Yes
Symene CLT, Bridport	Dorset	Formally constituted, working up scheme	Allotments	Yes
Witherslack Community Property Trust	Cumbria	Formally constituted, working up scheme	Pub and community shop	Yes

Source: As of 15 July 2012, as recorded on www.communitylandtrusts.org.uk

able to take forward its plans for community-based development – in opposition to market-led commercial proposals – due to the purchase of the site. It did this with a £1 million loan from the Greater London Enterprise Board and the Greater London Council; this has now been repaid, and further developments are funded by commercial loans repaid out of rental income, venue hire and fees. CSCB is a company limited by guarantee, controlled by a board where only local residents can become board members. All profits are ploughed back into the area rather than distributed.

The developed area now comprises 220 homes at affordable rents run by four mutual housing cooperatives. Coin Street Secondary Housing Cooperative is an Industrial and Provident Society established in 1987 to promote, develop and support housing cooperatives by providing advice, training and management services. In addition there are shops, galleries, restaurants, cafes and bars, a park, sports facilities and a community centre. The area has also been designed to open up the riverside to pedestrians and to provide pathways connecting the river to its hinterland. In addition CSCB runs a social enterprise, Coin Street Centre Trust, providing childcare, educational opportunities and enterprise support.

There are, however, plenty of less famous examples.

The East London Community Land Trust was also born out of community activism, but now specialises in providing affordable housing across East London. They are working to establish a CLT on the former site of St Clement's Hospital in Mile End with the support of the Greater London Authority. Boris Johnson, Mayor of London, signed a Mayoral Decision on 16 July 2012 to confirm this. Following a tender process, this Mayoral Decision will result in a partnership with the developers Galliford Try to restore the historic building and to provide housing that is 'permanently affordable', that is, not put for sale on the open market but kept in the ownership of the CLT and rented out at prices determined by household income. The freehold of the building and land will be transferred to the CLT once the building is restored, and Linden Homes (a subsidiary company of the developer) will administer the commercial elements of the development under a long lease from the CLT. Ground rents will then be available for reinvestment.

Meanwhile, in the Lake District, the Cumbria CLT Project is supporting Keswick Community Housing Trust in developing 10 affordable homes (in a notoriously high-cost housing market due to the pressures of tourism and the restrictions on development in a National Park). This initiative resulted from campaigning by Churches Together on the problem of local housing need. The land was made available by St John's Church (that had been gifted the land by Lodore Estates, originally as a burial site), and with the agreement of the Diocese to a £100,000 valuation. The organisation was constituted as an Industrial and Provident Society but charitable status is currently delaying development, so this may be changed. They are working in partnership with Cumbria Rural Housing Trust and Derwent and Solway Housing Association to build the properties.

And so on....

The 2011 Localism Act encourages the wider use of such development trust and CLT vehicles to enable local communities to promote development that meets their needs. The key factors to success appear to be the willingness of local residents to put in considerable time and effort to get the project to work, together with professional advice and support and, centrally, the ability to access land at relatively low cost. This last point is returned to below.

Self-build and plotlands

The above examples have tended to involve professional, if not commercial, developers working alongside community organisations. There is the possibility, however, of using community labour or 'sweat equity' to self-build properties. The idea of self-build on a privately bought plot has never been as popular in the UK as some other countries. Perhaps the rapid industrialisation of the UK encouraged predominantly commercial building in urban areas. There have, however, been some examples of self-build activity.

Plotlands are one such historic example.[21] These began in the 1870s, but with further waves after demobilisation in the First World War and again after the Second World War. The idea was to use marginal agricultural land, which had a low value, to enable low-income families to build basic houses for leisure purposes, and as a retreat from the conditions of the city. However, the dwellings tended to be extended and improved, and were increasingly used for more permanent living.

The planning legislation of 1947 stopped this because any such works would have required permission; the new town of Basildon was designated partly to deal with the plotlands of Pitsea and Laindon and to regularise them within conventional urban development. And indeed such plotlands can be romanticised. The buildings standards were often very poor and adequate sewerage and water supply missing. One remaining plotland – Jaywick – is notorious for its levels of deprivation, although views of residents vary between those who would like to see it completely replaced and those who argue that some investment in improvements would suffice.

Certainly this kind of unplanned development by lower-income and often marginal groups may be viewed with hostility by the state and other social groups, much in the way that travellers' sites are. To quote an online commentary:[22]

> Plotlands are a rare manifestation of unfettered working class creative expression. Outsider architecture, their random chaos is the very antithesis of the controlled and manicured English landscape. Starting with basic materials and plenty of ingenuity, a plotland house can grow into an amalgam of just about any architectural style imaginable. Pebbledash meets pirate ship, via gnomes, palm trees and Corinthian columns. The remaining plotlands are insular places that many people don't visit or even know about. Whilst there is an intense community spirit, there are often problems with crime, poverty and dilapidation. But people on the plotlands hold on, adding quirky personal touches to their shacks, handing them down to their children and grandchildren, who now have to contend with living in hastily thrown together buildings that were never meant to last more than a few years, let alone 80.

What such development did offer was the ability to build a home at low cost. Telling the story of Mr and Mrs Mills who built a bungalow at Dunton Hills, Essex, Ian Abley narrates how they bought the freehold of their plot for £20 in 1934 (equivalent to £1,073 in 2009). They got a mortgage of £2,414 for building materials and started with two rooms and a hall, expanding it as they went. They included a workshop and Mr Mills, a carpenter, traded from there, untrammelled by the need for any permission to do so.[23]

Colin Ward argues that the same idea motivated groups who took over vacant local authority properties, using their own labour to improve them and turning them, eventually, into housing cooperatives.[24] More recently, eco-builders have used self-build models to promote developments with a low impact on ecosystems. Pickerell's research has identified some examples, but also highlighted the problems that such radical forms of building currently face in terms of getting planning permission and ensuring compliance with building regulations.[25] She also points out that the CLT model can often be a useful vehicle for these innovative forms of development.

Overall self-build remains a very small proportion of total new housing supply: 14,000 dwellings in 2008. This amounted to 7 per cent of new build in England, 8 per cent in Scotland, 4 per cent in Wales but 25 per cent in Northern Ireland.[26] There have been government moves to encourage self-build, albeit on a restricted scale. In May 2012 a £30 million fund for self-build was launched, aiming to finance about 50 schemes in England.[27] This will provide short-term finance to part-fund land purchase and early construction costs such as material purchase. Up to 75 per cent of costs may be covered with the loan repaid on completion, thus assuming that some form of mortgage can be arranged on the completed dwellings.

It has been suggested that there are three roles that local government can play in supporting such self-build schemes. First, they can provide a site divided up into self-build plots, along the lines of the Almere project in the Netherlands or the Baugruppen activities in Freiburg, Germany.[28] Second, they can allocate sites without directly providing them. Department for Communities and Local Government guidance is now that local authorities should assess the local demand for self-build and allocate land for this form of development. And third, they can (subject to central government guidance) classify self-build housing as 'affordable' and thus zero-rated for the purposes of the CIL (see Chapter 2). These could form part of a package of tools and approaches that the planning system could adopt to support these new models of development. The remainder of this chapter discusses these.

Finding low-value land

The key to the successful exercise of these alternative models of development is to access low-value land so that the costs of the development are kept low, and the community reaps the benefit of increases in land value over time. The issue is how to acquire such land.

Using the public estate

One option is to use land from the public estate, preferably releasing it at a price below market value. As discussed above, the TCPA consider this to be a useful way of reviving the Garden City model for the 21st century. The public estate has been subject to a long-term programme of disposal in order to raise funds. *The state of the estate* report published in May 2012 showed that this was continuing, with a reduction in the worth of central government property estate by £278 million in 2010/11 alone.[29] This leaves a central government estate worth £120 billion, compared with a local authority estate of £250 billion.[30]

Central government has acknowledged that there is potential for releasing some of this property for use by communities and SMEs. However, this is dependent on central and local government developing a strategy for rationalising their estate that identifies properties that can be released. It also raises important questions about the terms on which such properties can be released. If the aim is simply to raise public sector funds, then the tendency will be to look for the highest value buyer and even to continue holding property if the market seems particularly weak at any specific time. However, SMEs and community groups may not be able to pay the hypothetically highest market value, and thus a different disposal strategy will be needed for potentially surplus public property to be made available to meet local property needs through community development and self-build. This contrasts with the situation of, say, military sites in the US that are no longer needed for operational activities. Under the work of the Defense Base Closure and Realignment Commission (BRAC), such sites are offered to the local community (through the local authority) at military land use (and hence relatively low) values for redevelopment and re-use.[31]

The government, under the Localism agenda, has heralded a new Community Right to Reclaim land as a way of communities gaining access to land owned by public bodies that is under-used. This builds on a pre-existing right under the 1980 Local Government Planning and Land Act called a PROD, or Public Request to Order Disposal. This applied to land in England and Wales owned by local authorities and certain public bodies, but has now been extended to government departments. Under its provisions, an individual can try and force a public landowner to take action over derelict or under-used publicly owned land by sending a formal request to the Secretary of State, who will then take the decision on whether or not to order disposal . Any such disposal does, however, occur again in the open market, and thus at open market value. This may create difficulties for community-based organisations in terms of raising the funds for such an open market purchase.

A community can also request a local authority to compulsorily purchase any property that is under-used, but local authorities are often rather reluctant to use powers that are quite time-consuming and resource-intensive to operate. If the local authority does purchase such a site, provision still has to be made to transfer the asset to the community. Once again, there are rules that require the local authority to get the best value for any asset that they sell, and thus these sales will again be in the open market. Finally, the government currently, as at various times in the past, is committed to advertising details of surplus publicly owned land and building so that communities – but also developers, of course – are able to consider the possibility of their purchase, again in the open market. Chapter 9 considers some means of community fundraising to enable such purchases to proceed, but the issue of the requirement for these sales to be conducted at open market values remains an important barrier.

Using planning policy

Given these difficulties in purchasing land, even public sector land, at a price that enables community-based development, this raises the question of whether the planning system can be used to restructure land prices within the local market.

The so-called exceptions policy is one way of doing this. As outlined in earlier chapters, when planning permission is granted for development on a site, the value of that site usually increases, sometimes quite substantially. This is particularly the case if agricultural land is granted permission for development, whether residential, retail or commercial, when it will increase in value not by a percentage but by several multiples. But even a change in development permission from a low-value use – say, light industry – to a higher-value use – say, commercial development or dense residential development – will result in a considerable uplift in value.

An exceptions policy retains a general policy of restricting such development opportunities in an area, thus keeping the land at the lower existing use values, but will grant planning permission *as an exception* for development that meets local needs.[32] This policy has been successfully used in rural areas to allow housing development in the green belt or areas subject to countryside protection policies where that housing is then only made available to local households, usually at lower prices or rents. Wider application of such exceptions policies for community-based development using these alternative vehicles would be a way of enabling land to pass at a value that does not represent the highest market development value of a site in the area. In effect the policy creates a separate sub-market in land for community-based development. In rural areas, this could be combined with the landowning farmer becoming a formal member within the CLT, thus contributing a share of the increment in land value to residential development value.

This approach was sought by residents in Basildon living in ex-plotlands that were now within the designated green belt. Such a designation would prevent any further development, but reallocating the land for development would result in a substantial uplift in land value. Therefore the residents wanted an exceptions policy to allow infill development to occur, to densify the plotlands area and to build out plots of undeveloped land. However, the local council in this case considered that such an infill policy would create a precedent for other development in the green belt and thus resisted it.

The role of precedent in the planning system is addressed in later chapters, including Chapter 9. But the central point to appreciate is the importance of an exception policy being drawn up within a local plan. The application of these exceptions policies could then happen on an ad hoc basis, as local communities find sites that they wish to develop, provided that the general policy is firmly stated in local plan documents.

An alternative approach is to reconsider the nature of current site allocation policies within the British planning system. Colin Ward has argued that a more relaxed form of planning is needed to allow initiatives such as plotlands to flourish. However, in his own inimitable style, he warned that this implies a major cultural shift:[33]

> Unofficial settlements are seen as a threat to wildlife, which is sacrosanct. The planning system is the vehicle that supports four-wheel-drive Range Rovers, but not the local economy, and certainly not those travellers and settlers seeking their own modest place in the sun. These people have bypassed the sacred rights of tenure, but still find their modest aspirations frustrated by the operations of planning legislation. Nobody actually planned such a situation. No professional planner would claim that his or her task was to grind unofficial housing out of existence, and nor would any of the local enforcers of the Building Regulations.

Much depends on how revised land allocation policies are drawn up. They could allow self-build policies or specifically permit eco-building schemes. Or they could favour development by any community-based organisation and then leave it to negotiation between the community-based organisation and local planners over the kind of development that would be appropriate. The key factor for revised site allocations to support community-based development – through not only granting development permission but also keeping site values low – is that the zoning should be restrictive to make it clear that the site is not available for general market development by a commercial developer. And if certain sites are restricted to community-based development, then it is important that site allocation occurs on the basis of discussion with local community organisations to ensure that appropriate sites are identified.

It should be recognised, however, that the contribution of the alternative modes of development reviewed here will be constrained unless there is a major value shift in their favour. However, some such shift, whether towards these alternative models and/or a return to public housebuilding, is essential to meet housing need. In either case, this will require land allocations through the planning system to support an enhanced level of low-cost housing provision.

EIGHT

Protecting and improving existing places

It is the essence of the growth-dependent approach to planning that it considers increases in the prices of land and buildings to be an indicator of success in planning a locality. Yet there are all sorts of buildings, spaces and places that are important to towns and cities and that contribute to the liveability of urban areas and yet have a relatively low economic value. Indeed, because of their lower economic value, they have a particularly important role to play in the lives of lower-income households and can contribute to the sustainability of places in a variety of ways. This chapter looks at what the planning system can do to keep such buildings, spaces and places available to meet the needs of all groups within existing communities, and to improve their quality without losing this availability to lower-income groups.

This chapter begins by looking at how the planning system can protect existing land uses from (re)development where this is needed in order to protect existing communities. It considers the use of planning regulation, both as a direct means of restraining development pressures and as a way of restructuring land and property markets to ensure low-value land uses are not driven out by higher ones. This involves closer consideration of the role of planning regulation and how it is supported by policies in plans, and develops the discussion began in Chapter 7. It then goes on to consider how existing land uses and places can be enhanced. Two aspects are covered: the improvement of building standards including energy efficiency; and the improvement of local areas, including residential and also town centres, with their important retail functions and spaces for SME premises. The chapter concludes by considering policies in relation to vacant land and property, looking at housing, commercial property and sites.

Protecting existing land uses from development pressures

Regulating development proposals

It has been shown that the most problematic aspects of growth-dependent planning come to the fore when existing land uses and even communities are displaced by new market-led development. This suggests the need for the planning system to be able to protect these sites, places and neighbourhoods. To date the tool that is available to achieve this is rather limited and even crude in application, with considerable unintended consequences. Planning regulation is the main means of protection from development pressures. Such regulation takes a number of interrelated forms. To begin with, there is the baseline requirement to get planning permission for almost all new development, including changes of use. This clearly provides the potential for permission to be refused and thus new development to be resisted.

Such regulation can be enhanced by additional sets of considerations and requirements in the case of historic buildings, important trees and conservation areas of historical importance or specific character with regard to the built environment. Restrictions on development may also be applicable in the case of sites of nature conservation importance as habitats and/or parts of ecosystems and – largely relevant outside of urban areas – where landscape value, access to and enjoyment of the countryside is concerned.

Indeed the number of different bases on which opposition to new development can be justified often gives the impression that the planning system is largely about managing and nuancing such restrictions. This is clearly the complaint of many developers, large and small. However, as set out in Chapter 2, there are caveats to the view of the planning system as inherently restrictive of urban development. There is the operation of planning instruments such as the General Permitted Development Order and the Use Classes Order, which permit certain developments (including certain changes of use) to proceed without the need for planning permission,[1] and further, there is the general presumption in favour of (sustainable) development, as set out in the NPPF[2] and hence in conforming local and neighbourhood plans, which will affect the decisions on individual planning applications. These undermine the potential to protect low-value land uses.

So how might these uses be protected?

One immediate possibility is the use of planning regulation to prevent existing low-value land uses, including housing areas, from being redeveloped for higher-value uses. There are two issues involved here. The first concerns the influence of such communities on the regulatory process. The second is about the limitations of current planning regulation to deliver a satisfactory outcome, even if such voices are listened to.

Community engagement over regulatory decisions is essential in judging whether existing land uses should be protected or not. It may be that, taking the views of the community as a whole, redevelopment is what is desired. However, the history of demolition and redevelopment of lower-value residential areas suggests that often communities want the planning system to protect and enhance what is already there. It is important that the voices of these groups are heard within local debates about the planning of the area. The problem of socially vulnerable and environmental interests having less of a voice within planning debates, however, is one that has been referred to already and is a major preoccupation within planning studies. It seems that if opportunities for participation in planning decision making is opened up, it is inevitable that those communities with more time, resources and knowledge of the system will take a disproportionate amount of the planners' time and resources, and be more effective in defending the amenities that such higher-income groups have already acquired. Considerable effort is required to give lower-income groups a greater say within such decision making in order to achieve pathways to just sustainability.

This is not just an issue of process. There are structural features of the planning system that prevent the views of more vulnerable groups being prioritised. There are limited grounds on which planning permission can be refused, and these tend to focus on land uses rather than the specific social needs that a land use fulfils. Planning control is currently limited to regulating new development and changes of land uses. It cannot control shifts within a land use such as where a multiple or high-end retailer takes over from a discount shop or tourist-oriented retailing takes over from a local butcher or bakery. The planning system thus does not have the legitimacy to distinguish between different social groups and therefore apply different decisions to similar land uses used by different social groups. Yet this is necessary if the ability of lower-income groups to use planning regulation to resist unwanted development is to be distinguished from the NIMBYism of higher-income groups resisting development so that they may continue to enjoy their already enhanced local amenities.

This suggests that thought needs to be given to how lower-income areas in need of protection from development pressures can be identified in plan documents as particular foci of planning regulation. What is needed is the possibility that planning regulation can distinguish and then protect the specific assets and land uses that support the lifestyles of lower-income groups and contribute, in this way, to just sustainability. The planning system needs to be able to differentiate between protection of an urban garden used for food production by low-income groups to support healthier and cheaper diets, say, and a gated urban space that provides an amenity setting for high-income housing.

It may be that particular resources can be channelled into neighbourhood planning for such areas, but it may also be necessary to create new forms of planning regulation. This suggests the creation of a category of, say, 'community asset supporting just sustainability', which can be used as a basis for regulatory decision making. Creating such a basis for planning decisions will not necessarily overcome local conflicts concerning a development proposal, even within a single affected social group, but it will offer some protection for land uses that contribute to local needs and could contribute to more sustainable urban outcomes.

By contrast, the current changes to planning regulation are relaxing certain aspects of planning control and allowing market processes to determine land uses. Five such changes are occurring (see Table 8.1 for details of the Use Classes Order):[3]

- for a three-year period, offices (B1A) can be converted to residential (C3);

Table 8.1: Use Classes Order, 2012/13

A1 Shops	B1 Business	C1 Hotels
A2 Financial and professional services	B2 General industrial	C2 Residential institutions
A3 Restaurants and cafes	B3 Storage or distribution	C2A Secure residential institutions
A4 Drinking establishments	D1 Non-residential institutions	C3 Dwelling houses
A5 Hot food takeaways	D2 Assembly and leisure	C4 Houses in multiple occupation
Sui Generis a variety of uses such as theatres, launderettes, scrapyards, casinos, etc		

Source: www.plainview.co.uk

- temporary changes of use are permitted for two years initially between shops (A1), financial and professional services (A2), restaurants and cafes (A3) and business (B1);
- empty spaces above shops can be converted into two rather than just one flat;
- there is more scope for householder development without requirement planning consent; and
- agricultural buildings can change use to other non-residential uses.

Such relaxation of regulation is often opposed, almost in principle. However, not all existing patterns of land use are desirable to maintain or, less strongly, necessary to maintain. Where economic growth or restructuring in desirable directions is occurring, changes of land uses can promote positive outcomes. Some degree of flexibility is essential for urban change.

But market conditions can be such as to render relaxation of regulation inimical to local well-being. As emphasised here, sometimes low-value land uses fulfil important local social and economic functions. This would be the case with small offices for SMEs or self-employed people who would find their premises threatened by the profitability of residential development in some locations, driving a change of use and associated refurbishment. In other locations, where there is surplus and unoccupied office space, the relaxation may reduce costs sufficiently at the margin to encourage much-needed residential development.

Restructuring land markets

While planning regulation has a key role to play in restricting specific development proposals and thus protecting existing land uses of community value, it also has a more general role to play. This relates to the way that such regulation can structure local land markets. The emphasis here is not on the regulation of individual development proposals, but rather the effect on the land markets of clearly established policies for what development will be permitted where across a locality.

The pattern of local land values across a locality depends on the interrelationship of the distribution of permitted land uses under the operation of the planning system, with the distribution of market pressures for development. The land value of any site will result from the combination of the permitted land use with the highest value interpretation of that use by market actors, since competition within land and development markets tends to push sites towards the 'highest and best' land use, that is, the most valuable in market terms. A clear indication of what kinds of land uses and developments will be permitted will thus help to shape local land markets. A plan that sets these out will help bring land values into alignment with market valuations of these permitted land uses. However, there are two considerations to take into account.

The first is the certainty with which development actors and landowners assume that the land allocations will or will not be turned into planning permissions. A zoning system, whereby development permission is automatically granted once the zoning plan is approved, is most likely to structure the local land market in a way that maps prices onto permitted uses. However, the UK system is not a zoning system but requires individual planning applications, and each is judged on its merits, having regard to the local plan and also 'other material considerations'. This means that any individual planning application may be deemed unacceptable and turned down, but it also means that there is always the possibility of getting development permission on a site that appears to be allocated for another land use.

Indeed, under the UK system, there are strong incentives to push for planning permission on sites that are not explicitly allocated in plans. This gives developers additional profits from buying land more cheaply than would be the case with sites that are so allocated, and it also allows local landowners to capture a bit of this 'hope' value, that is, the gap between current use value of the land and the value with planning permission. Both developers and landowners are, therefore, likely to push the boundaries of what is identified as permissible development in a local plan. The solution to this is to exercise planning regulation more tightly in conformity with the plan and to try to avoid such off-plan developments. But there are other issues concerning the detailed nature of the planning regulation policies that may be set out in local plans.

This goes back to the fine-grain of how planning regulation works, explored in the preceding chapter and above. If planning consent is given for a site to be converted or developed to a fairly broad category of land use – residential or even employment-generating – then the market will operate its competitive dynamics in order to select the most profitable and highest value use for that site. There is no economic rationale not to seek to develop the more profitable kind of new housing or to choose a commercial over an industrial use for an employment-generating site. If local plans are to structure local land markets in ways that support land uses meeting local needs through lower-value activities, different kinds of planning regulation policies are needed.

There are five issues to consider here: linking planning permission to occupier and not just land use; using scale as a basis for planning regulation; supporting higher densities of development in some circumstances; readdressing the role of mixed-use developments; and reconsidering how precedent shapes planning regulation. Each of these will be discussed in turn (Chapter 10 collects these points together with others made through the book on planning regulation to propose a collection of reforms).

As discussed above, a major limitation of the current planning system is the linking of specific planning permissions to relatively crude categories of land use, nuanced only by the planning gain that can be negotiated and the conditions attached. It was argued that it would be helpful for the agenda of planning for just sustainability if it was possible to reject a planning application because it would replace a land use that was of value to local communities through its contribution to justice and sustainability. In the context of considering how planning regulation helps to structure a local land market, it can also be argued that it would help promote this agenda if planning permissions could relate to the nature of the occupier and not just the land use.

A good example of this argument comes from work on planning for the provision of premises for SMEs, that is, affordable workplaces. Ferm's research has examined such planning in detail.[4] She looked at policies that sought to use planning gain to deliver affordable workspaces as part of new developments. She identified a range of problems in line with the underlying limitations of growth-dependent planning. The planning policies encouraging mixed-use development (which included the provision of affordable workspaces within a broadly residential development) were actually crowding out existing low-value business space. In practice, they favoured certain types of activity, such as creative businesses, and did not meet the needs of start-ups, young businesses, low-value manufacturers and small family-run retail and service businesses.

Affordability was often interpreted in a way that did not meet the needs of many local businesses, that is, rents were just too high, and could only be ensured in the short term due to the operation of market dynamics after the first letting or sale. The Section 106 agreements tended only to stipulate short-lease terms and the cost to the workspace provider rather than the tenant, which did not ensure that local low-value businesses would benefit. In general these policies tended to support certain types of businesses that would lead to further gentrification of an area rather than economic diversity of business activity. She argued that the way to avoid this was to use not-for-profit workspace providers, that is, aim the spaces at particular types of occupier; this could be supported by more targeted planning regulation if it was permissible for the occupier of the property to be specified.

In the retail sector, Westminster City Council in London uses an area-based variant of this approach by specifying certain uses very tightly, effectively linking them to specific categories of occupiers.[5] Their Special Policy Areas policy is used in relatively small areas, such as a street, where they are seeking to protect small areas of distinctive land uses from other forms of development. This is currently used to protect the traditional men's tailoring area of Savile Row. However, the operation of the Use Classes Order means that this protection is rather limited, an indicative rather than a regulatory policy. It would require planning reforms to enable new developments from other kinds of user to be rejected. If this was possible, it would effectively constrain the value of property in these streets.

A second way that planning regulation could work to restructure land markets to protect low-value land uses would be to have policies that constrained the size of new developments and conversions. In Italy retail planning policy used to operate to favour small-scale units and restrict larger units, particularly in town centres. This could be adopted in the British context to protect smaller stores from redevelopment into major multiples units, and this would also alter the land values for areas with smaller units, often the secondary and tertiary shopping locations.

Density policies are a well-established planning tool, but the way that they operate to incentivise development and affect land values is complicated. Encouraging higher densities of development is broadly favoured as a way of creating more sustainable urban forms and thereby enabling shorter journey distances, use of walking and cycling as modes of transport and greater patronage of local services (although it is also widely recognised that orienting such developments around public transport nodes and routes is essential). But higher-density development also has other advantages. Denser development, *ceteris paribus*, is more profitable development and allows greater opportunity for planning gain, as Chapter 3 explained. It also offers the prospects of a greater quantum of development that could offset the effects of policies that are restricting new developments, even if in the name of protecting assets and land uses that are of value to communities and support local sustainability. And such development is likely to comprise smaller units, which may then command lower prices.

In the US higher-density residential developments of smaller units are typically sold at the lower end of the market, and lower-density policies are often used to socially engineer the occupancy of new residential areas towards higher-income households.

Fourth, policies that require mixed uses restructure local land markets in interesting ways. They can encourage the mixing of different social groups with consequent impacts on local areas through demand for services. The requirement in London under the Livingstone Mayoralty for a high proportion of a residential site to be developed for affordable housing had this effect. It has been criticised for creating fewer new social housing units than would have been the case if these units were developed off-site; however, it did create greater integration of social areas by building more social housing units within areas of high private sector demand. However, this example, and the discussion of Ferm's work above, makes it clear that mixed-use policies need to operate in conjunction with planning regulation that is able to specify, to some extent, the nature of the occupancy of new development.

Finally there is the role that precedent plays within planning regulation. One problem that arises with the exercise of planning regulation is the concern that a decision taken on a specific development may create a precedent for future decision making. Rather than link the regulatory decision to past regulatory decisions, the current impact on specific social groups, particularly more vulnerable local groups, needs to be more heavily weighted.

This discussion of planning regulation differs from that of alternative mechanisms for generating new development in the last chapter because it is largely hypothetical. These are reforms that it would seem desirable to put in place, rather than examples of alternative development activity that is happening or has happened in the past. There is therefore scope for considerably more debate about such regulatory reforms, for fine-tuning proposals and considering how they fit with planning law. However, the argument here is that some reform of planning regulation is essential if community needs are to be met and a just sustainability agenda progressed.

Much of this discussion has been about protecting areas and sites from the pressures for market-led development that growth-dependent planning would encourage. However, in situations of weak economic demand, the position facing the planning system in trying to promote just sustainability is quite different. There will be no shortage of spaces that can be made available for lower-value uses and there may even be vacancies across all sectors. The growth-based planning approach to this situation is not to celebrate the availability of low-value opportunities but rather to try and attract development into an area; however, low market demand may constrain the effectiveness of this approach. The rest of this chapter explores some specific alternative approaches.

Improving housing standards

Chapter 6 made it clear that adequate housing standards were a key element of a planning agenda aimed at well-being and just sustainability. It also pointed out the current inadequacies in the housing stock. Measures for tackling such problems of standards generally require a mix of subsidies for improvements to public and private housing stock, combined with regulations requiring these standards to be adhered to. Regulation is particularly important in the private rented stock, although the weak economic position of many tenants (including students, recent immigrants and those on housing benefit) can make it difficult to implement and enforce these regulations effectively.

An aspect of housing standards that demonstrates the close links between social and environmental sustainability concerns thermal comfort and the need to tackle fuel poverty. Here there is scope for improving the standard of housing and at the same time achieving improved energy efficiencies that reduce the costs of energy bills and also carbon emissions.[6] Here subsidies are, by and large, the adopted policy approach, although there have been problems of take-up even among lower-income households that have been entitled to direct grants rather than partial subsidies and loans; there are also concerns over the potential for current policy approaches to be regressive in their overall impact.[7]

In some cases, a more collective approach to such improvements has been adopted. A good example is provided by the Brent Housing

Partnership (BHP) which has sought to upgrade energy efficiency on the Brentfield Estate off (and partly on) the North Circular Road in Neasden, Brent. This involves installing external insulation cladding to 114 homes and photovoltaic (PV) tiles to 84 of these, in total covering a third of the houses on the estate. Loft insulation and double-glazed windows and doors are also being fitted together with new roofs using a Marley ecologic roof tile that removes nitrogen oxide pollutants. Given the road-side location, this is an innovative way to improve local air quality.[8]

This follows the experience with more general area improvement. General Improvement Areas were a policy of the 1960s and 1970s that sought to improve the collective facilities, street scene and the fabric of individual houses in an attempt to improve standards without recourse to redevelopment.[9] The difficulty with this policy, however, was that it could become a pathway to gentrification. It proved challenging to find a way to make such improvements without the benefits becoming internalised in higher prices and rents. Curran and Hamilton have coined the term 'just green enough' to suggest the kinds of environmental improvements that do not lead to gentrification;[10] discussing a specific US case study, they state (p 1028):

> Ideally, cleanup of Newtown Creek will be just green enough to improve the health and quality of life of existing residents, but not so literally green as to attract upscale 'sustainable' LEED-certified residential developments that drive out working-class residents and industrial businesses.

They argue for an emphasis on the less visible aspects of area improvement that are less likely to feed through to price increases through the operation of market demand. Energy efficiency improvements may well be one of these measures given that they do not seem to significantly affect prices or rents.

Town centre enhancement

Lower-value shopping has a strong spatial dimension. What counts as secondary and tertiary shopping is usually defined by its location. Prime retail property will be found in the main part of the shopping centre – whether a town centre or a shopping mall – with the greater pedestrian footfall, and is usually identified by the presence of a major multiple retailer, such as Marks & Spencer or Boots the Chemist, surrounded by other multiples. Secondary shopping will be further from this location in the town centre, or down side aisles in a shopping mall. It will be characterised by more non-retail uses – including betting offices and estate agents – and more independent shops. Tertiary shopping is even further away, down side roads or forming separate neighbourhood parades. As might be expected from this terminology, tertiary retail units are worth less in market rents and prices than secondary units, and these are worth less than units in prime locations.

The key question is how this differentiation of retail outlets meets the need for shopping across a local community. There is, of course, a tendency for more expensive and non-everyday shopping opportunities to be disproportionately represented in prime locations. Discount outlets are more likely to be found in secondary or even tertiary sites. There is considerable debate over whether more local shopping actually imposes a greater cost for an equivalent basket than multiple outlets that may be found in higher-value locations.[11] However, there is clearly a benefit to offering a range of shopping opportunities to meet a variety of needs. This is something that growth-dependent planning misses as it strives to encourage local economic development through attracting high market-value outlets. A study of the research looking at secondary shopping showed a general failure to appreciate the importance of lower-value shopping.[12]

Central government policy has tended to focus heavily on a unified sense of the 'health' of shopping centres in which indicators of prime rental values and vacancies have been given priority. The 1993 Planning Policy Guidance Note No 6 (PPG6) referred exclusively to shop vacancies in prime areas in measuring the vitality and viability of centres; the 1996 version did extend this to consider vacancies but not rents in secondary areas. From 1996 onwards the concern with town centres has been set in the context of the sequential test that sought to shift new development back into central locations. It required that new retail facilities be located first in town centres, then in edge-of-centre locations, and then in district and local centres before edge-of-town locations.

While there has been some growing appreciation of the need to have a diversity of shopping facilities, success in planning terms remains an absence of vacancies in shopping frontages together with rising rents. This is, again, the growth-dependent approach in action. There is instead a need to plan for and protect a wide range of shopping units including as assessed in rental or price terms. A report by CB Hillier Parker highlights the problem with the way that planning policies and regulation currently work. They argue:[13]

> Currently, 'planners' objectives' as expressed in Local Plans are substantially based on resisting or at least controlling change. Thus most Local Plans define prime and secondary shopping frontages; and then have policies along the lines of 'planning permission will not be granted for changes of use or developments which would result in more than x% of properties in the prime frontages and y% in the secondary shopping frontages being occupied by non A1 retail uses'. Non-retail uses are thus seen as disadvantageous – mainly because they are perceived as breaking the continuity of the browsing experience for the shopper, and resulting in dead frontage or cut-off points beyond which shoppers will not go. Of course, this is a simplistic response, which ignores the fact that many non-retail uses are substantial generators of pedestrian traffic in their own right, for example cafe/bar units, or banks and building societies. It also usually takes little account of the functional relationship and linkages between the prime and secondary shopping areas in individual town centres.

So what more appropriate policies could be introduced?

The National Retail Planning Forum (NRPF) has put forward some suggestions.[14] For example, they note that public realm improvement schemes rarely cover secondary areas, nor do they extend to smaller district and neighbourhood centres. This could be the focus of specific projects, either location-specific or targeted at neighbourhood parades, say. For example, there was an area in Seven Sisters Road, London, which was off the main shopping high street but included the entrance to a covered market and several discount shops. It was also the location for several bus stops and the existing seating had become a gathering place for alcoholics, which was a nuisance for the shoppers and also the schoolchildren waiting for buses. The seating was altered, and with some other minor adjustments this became a useful public space. Another example is the seating project invested in by Haringey Borough Council, which provides small benches along the hail-and-ride sections of a local bus stop, including by neighbourhood parades. Again this small amenity adds to the use value and convenience of the parades. The NRPF also draw attention to the lack of maintenance of shop fronts in secondary locations. An example of the difference this can make is the investment – admittedly in advance of the Olympic Games – in a secondary shopping street in Leyton, East London, with new street furniture and painted shopfronts.[15]

More generally there is a need to recognise the importance of lower-value retail areas in all planning decision making. For example, the W12 Centre in Shepherds Bush, London, provides an example of how a rather different idea of what constitutes a successful shopping centre may be needed. Shepherds Bush has been transformed in recent years by the opening of the Westfield Shopping Centre. This has brought considerable additional purchasing power into the locality with some spillover effects for local businesses, but it has also altered the competitive landscape for existing local shopping. Some have prospered, some have not. The W12 Centre was devised as a district shopping centre but it is now characterised by a couple of low-end multiples and discount shops together with a number of vacant units. A variety of uses have been devised to continue to bring life to the centre. Ziella Bryars talks of a free books project based in a now-empty McDonalds, which also houses a second-hand furniture showroom. There is a beauty salon in a space between units and a theatre piece took place in another empty unit.[16] However, such activities struggle in the face of a lack of local government support and a growth-dependent view of what constitutes retail success.

The NRPF are proposing that all Retail Impact Statements submitted by developers in support of planning applications include the impacts on secondary (and one might add, other) retail locations. They also argue that existing town centre management initiatives need to consider these areas alongside the core prime area, and understand the interconnections between different shopping localities that contribute to each performing to the level of profitability needed to keep them in business.

The recent Portas project, headed up by retail consultant and media personality Mary Portas, is an intriguing mix of a conventional nod to growth-dependent planning and more creative ideas.[17] In part, it seeks to bring market-led economic development to town centres and creates the usual markers of success in terms of reduced vacancy rates but also rising rents. But in part, it is suggesting an alternative and more diverse vision of what a retail area can be. Following the initial report, the project sought bids from town centres to become a Portas pilot, which would yield them relatively modest funding of £100,000 on average together with advice and support from central government and retail industry leaders and peer learning from the network of Portas pilots. Over 370 applications were made and 12 were selected, each with a rather different focus. A further 12 pilots are due to be announced, with three more in London funded by the Greater London Authority. Supplementary measures announced by the government include a £1 million Future High Street X-Fund for 'creative and effective schemes' for town centres, a National Markets Day and Fortnight and a £500,000 Business Improvements Districts Fund to help town centres access set-up loans. Helpful as this may be for non-prime areas, recent reports suggest there are problems of implementation with the programme that need to be addressed.

Box 8.1: The first 12 Portas Pilots

- Bedford, Bedfordshire: mentoring support and community use of empty properties
- Croydon, London: creating a market, food and cultural quarter in an area affected by the 2011 riots
- Dartford, Kent: starting a school for shopkeepers and opening up spaces for use by community organisations
- Bedminster, Bristol: bicycle rickshaw service, review of parking and a focus on street art and street theatre
- Liskeard, Cornwall: guerrilla gardening, yarn bombing and arts scene
- Margate, Kent: educational courses, job club services, pop-up shops
- Market Rasen, Lincolnshire: restoring market town look, free parking, mentoring
- Nelson, Lincolnshire: young persons' cafe, sports activities, new art and vintage market
- Newbiggin by the Sea, Northumberland: better branding, improving local transport, pop-up shops
- Stockport, Manchester: creative arts complex, outdoor screenings, new parking strategy, street champions
- Stockton on Tees, Teesside: live entertainment and markets to boost evening economy
- Wolverhampton, West Midlands: entrepreneurial support, joint branding and social media

One kind of retail outlet that was identified by the Portas review as particularly important in creating local economic activity is the local market. For a long time seen as rather old-fashioned, markets have now had a renaissance and can take many forms, from the traditional open-air produce market to covered areas of discount shopping to occasional farmers' markets and higher-value craft markets. These can be important in offering good value shopping aimed at everyday needs, although this is a rather different kind of market to the one focused on the occasional, tourist and leisure shopper. The difficulty is maintaining their value to existing communities.[18] An interesting example is the Teenage Market in Stockport which specifically provides facilities for younger people to sell products and items while at the same time offering an outlet for music and comedy performances. This initiative, which was spearheaded by 17-year-old Tom Barratt, also had the side-effect of giving younger people a sense of ownership of their urban area.[19] Research by Aiesha pinpoints the need to provide specific planning and management policies to support local markets.[20]

Spaces for small and medium-sized enterprises

SME premises are particularly at risk of redevelopment. They are low value and perceived of as back-room or left-over spaces. The current uses are often seen as temporary and readily able to be relocated, regardless of how long they have been there. These are small pieces in the urban jigsaw. Traditionally they have even been seen as bad neighbours and something that should be moved out to more orderly industrial and business spaces. This has been part of a tradition of separating land uses and zoning them into distinct areas. It is now recognised that mixed uses often contribute to greater vitality in settlements, and these non-residential uses can be part of the chain of value creation that supports local economic development.

However, Ferm's work has shown that there is some resistance to protecting such workspaces where they already exist, especially if redevelopment is a possibility.[21] This would require new forms of planning policy ready to support such existing uses and to reject redevelopment proposals even if this uplifted land values. If these uses are to contribute more fully to the local economy and perhaps lose some of the stigma associated with these untidy activities, they may require small-scale area improvements to the local environment. Negotiation between local residents and businesses on matters such as parking and deliveries as well as hours of operation may also make these workspaces better neighbours and build a stronger coalition for their continued existence *in situ*.

In addition Ferm found that many developers did not take this form of provision very seriously. The result of these policies tended to be a pepper-potting of small business space which failed to generate the local agglomeration economies that often makes local businesses viable. Ferm called for planning policies to protect employment land, preventing its replacement by mixed-use developments that actually had little local employment creation potential. Policies for incubator units for start-ups and young businesses and support of independent retail and service businesses could also be important.

Vacant property and land

So far this chapter has largely considered the management of existing properties, housing, shops and small workplaces. But there is also the potential, particularly for vacant property and land, to be brought in to use and to be of value to local communities.

Empty homes

Another potential source of lower-value housing comes from the re-use of empty housing. While any market will require a small degree of redundancy to work, and thus some empty properties are to be expected, the numbers in the UK are high and extend across the private and public sectors. Figures from 2011 suggest 720,000 empty homes in England, of which 279,000 have been empty for more than six months.[22] About 40 per cent are in the private sector, the remainder in largely council ownership. These statistics may, however, be an under-estimate as they do not always include homes that have become vacant because residents have moved out in anticipation of a regeneration scheme, or private sector schemes that have been left short of final completion because of a downturn affecting sales combined with the developer's desire to avoid incurring council tax on a completed dwelling.

The government created a £100 million fund as part of the 2010 Comprehensive Spending Review and made the re-use of empty properties an element of the Affordable Homes Programme within the 2011 Housing Strategy.[23] This has now (2013) been increased to £160 million, to be split between community and voluntary groups. But the figures that are projected for bringing empty homes into use are relatively modest, at around 11,000 homes by 2015. The Homes and Communities Agency's approach has been twofold. On the one hand it provides skills training, knowledge and support. There is a web-based Empty Homes Toolkit providing information and good practice examples. On the other, it has developed an interactive Geographic Information System (GIS)-based Empty Homes Mapping Toolkit, bringing together a variety of sources of information on empty homes at the Lower Super Output Area scale (that is, quite a detailed scale).

However, information and advice is unlikely to be sufficient. There are financial and landownership issues involved here. There have been a range of suggestions for how financial incentives can be altered to encourage the re-use of empty homes. The Royal Institution of Chartered Surveyors has argued that there is a perverse incentive operating whereby councils get an additional element in their annual grant from central government for every empty home, so that putting these homes back into use actually reduces council income, which then has to be actively recouped through council tax.[24] There are widespread calls for VAT on domestic refurbishments to be reduced to zero; works to empty homes currently attract only a reduced rate.[25] The Trades Union Congress has called for a higher rate of council tax to be levied on empty properties, a reform that the government is considering. In addition there are the advocates of Site Value Rating whereby all land is taxed according to its designated use even if currently vacant, to discourage buildings lying idle (although this runs the danger of promoting growth-dependent planning if taxation is linked to the highest possible market value).

It is also suggested that passing vacant properties into the hands of new owners could encourage their use. Local authorities can use an Empty Dwelling Management Order to act against owners who refuse to cooperate on bringing empty properties into use, particularly where the property is an eyesore or there is a danger to public safety, and they can exercise compulsory purchase powers to buy up properties.[26] Where some empty houses have been inherited, but the property needs work before being put on the market for occupation, local authority ownership could act as a means of doing this work, and then making the property available for occupation again. Or local neighbours could be empowered to buy a property or rent it for a time with a view to improving it and putting it to use. They have an incentive to do so as they will get some of the benefits of having a derelict property brought back into occupation;

but it may be that specific forms of mortgage funding are needed to facilitate this.

Empty commercial properties

Empty properties are taken as a key sign of the need for market-based planning, but they are also a sign of the failure of this approach. A number of initiatives have arisen that seek to provide useful occupation of such empty premises and thereby create a better local environment – since empty properties never enhance the local environment. It is argued that filling empty properties in this way also reduces security and insurance costs, as occupation acts as a form of protection for the property, and as an advertisement for the property, potentially leading to longer-term commercial occupation.

Shops have been a particular focus of this approach. In a 2010 report, the consultants SQW state that there were approximately 25,000 empty shops or 13 per cent of all UK retail units.[27] However, they also counted 250 temporary projects in progress, 75 per cent of which were in vacant shops. The other activities were in offices, housing, pubs, places of worship, car showrooms and building sites (more of which below). The Empty Shops Network provides a mix of advice, advocacy and help with administration to enable uses to occupy empty shops for a period from a few days to a couple of years. These 'pop-up' uses help create an active frontage and provide a useful service. They can also act as a catalyst to a new longer-term use of the property by showing that such occupation can be beneficial. There may also be some local economic benefits if, as is more likely, the pop-up occupier comes from the locality.

The Empty Shops Network is an interesting mix of straightforward business advice with a base in creative and community organisations. The original Pop Up People Project was an action research project, funded by the Arts Council of England with crowdfunding through High Street Hundred (more on crowdfunding in the next chapter). It ran a number of events during 2011–12 in different localities, demonstrating the potential of the pop-up phenomenon. The involvement of the Arts Council highlights that an important use for empty property can often be cultural events. The SQW report found that half of the temporary uses they researched were arts or culture related. Renew Australia, a key promoter of 'meanwhile uses', particularly emphasised this aspect and its founder, Marcus Westbury, has argued that such uses have been fundamental in reviving the city of Newcastle, Australia.[28]

Spitalfields Market in London is now a redeveloped space, following the growth-dependent model, with a range of retail outlets, cafes and new commercial buildings inside and around the refurbished historic market building. During the lengthy development process, during which the market stood near-derelict, a range of creative and temporary uses were housed on the site. Jackie Sadek says that this 'kept the name alive, while seriously populating Spitalfields – as a place and as an address – with some enduring brand values. It was smart. But it was expedient.'[29] She goes on to emphasise that while this policy has much to offer to developers, 'it must be community-focused....As well as the antiques and collectibles market, Spitalfields had a temporary swimming pool and towed an American aluminium trailer-diner onto site.' Taking a firmly commercial view, she argues that 'Temporary uses are cheaper, much quicker to implement, and may play a role in kick starting a place (if not the development immediately) and they can also often be moved from place to place as development comes forward in one place but not the next.'

This sees temporary use as complementary to a growth-dependent approach, a way of biding one's time until this approach is fully appropriate. However, it is possible to take a different approach which emphasises community-based uses; there is nothing, beyond the owner finding an alternative occupier, that prevents temporary use continuing for as long as the space is available. In their research, SQW identified a wide range of uses occurring: a social enterprise in an old bank testing new models of business support; a pilot for a maritime heritage centre which was then able to secure grant funding; workspaces in an empty warehouse for artists, craftspeople and creative start-ups; community shops; and a music mentoring scheme for young people.

One specific tool that encourages the use of empty shops in this way is the Meanwhile Lease.[30] This is a simplified, user-friendly lease that provides enough reassurance to landlords for them to permit the temporary use. It can also be framed as a Meanwhile Intermediary Lease to a local authority or community organisation together with Meanwhile Use Subleases so that the local authority or community organisation can promote and manage a specific temporary use or even a programme of such uses.

The key role that local planning can play here is to ease any regulatory constraints on such small-scale pop-up initiatives. In particular the operation of the Use Classes Order may act as a constraint since its raison d'être is to limit the uses that may be undertaken in a specific property. This was recognised by the Planning Minister in June 2011 when he indicated that 'meanwhile uses' would be encouraged where possible. The need for planning permission in order to temporarily change use was signalled as part of a reform of the Use Classes Order (see above). Another possible change that may be required is in parking policy, where the new temporary use has different requirements to the pre-existing one.

Local authorities can also persuade their estates departments to take a more flexible approach where their own property is involved. This may mean that they have to be willing to take on extra risks or do some refurbishment works to make the space usable. There can also be issues with regard to business rates on such properties. If a building is classified as uninhabitable, it is exempt from paying business rates; an owner is likely to have tried to persuade the Valuation Office that it is indeed uninhabitable, and a temporary use may threaten this. Again, some flexibility is required here.

An example of this has been the approach to encouraging housing above shops. These are likely to be lower-value housing units compared to other local properties and, furthermore, are likely to stay so even when repeatedly traded on the open market. There are currently capital allowances for flat conversions above shops provided that the rents charged fall below set limits, ensuring that they contribute to lower-priced supply. Planning policies could encourage such conversions by ensuring a speedy and positive response on planning applications. They could even consider taking such conversions out of planning regulation altogether through a local variation to permitted development under a Local Development Order. These measures might be more effective than the central agency to promote 'living over the shop' that was considered and then dismissed in the 2000s. This agency was to focus on providing advice and hand-holding, but as consultants asked to advise on the scheme concluded: 'The market is wary of the scheme.'[31]

> ### Box 8.2: Flat conversion allowances[32]
> - Available for conversion, renovation and repair of 'qualifying flats' and providing access to such flats.
> - Cannot be used for purchase of property rights.
> - Property must have been built before 1980.
> - The upper floors should have been unused or used only for storage for a year before works start.
> - They cannot be more than four storeys above the ground floor and must have been originally constructed primarily for residential use.
> - Ground floor must be authorised for business use.
> - Each new flat must be a self-contained dwelling with no more than four rooms.

Vacant land

Whereas the previous two sections have focused on empty buildings, there is also potential for re-use of empty sites that is somewhat different from their use for community-based development explored in the last chapter. Here the emphasis is on temporary use of empty sites, 'meanwhile uses'. Recognising that there may be gaps in the development processes by which sites move from one beneficial use to another, meanwhile uses are a way to ensure that these sites contribute to the quality of life in a locality.

While such uses may include occupation by local businesses, particularly start-ups, meanwhile use of land as opposed to building offers a different kind of opportunity. The land can be used for sports facilities such as football pitches. It can be turned into a wildlife reserve or an urban garden. And, providing the lease is for the length of a growing season, the land may be ideal for community food growing projects. If the quality of the soil on the sites is an issue for food growing, other gardening might be possible, or skips and other containers can be located on the site. As Chapter 6 outlined, such food growing projects have a range of benefits including the opportunity for exercise, improvement to diets with fresh produce and community building through creating a cooperative endeavour.

Where such sites are the subject of ongoing discussions between planners and developers on future development, then planners can encourage and even negotiate for a meanwhile use in the interim. Where there is no such proposal in prospect, local authorities could play a role in identifying suitable sites (in consultation with local communities) and then negotiating with landowners for such uses. The win-win nature of temporary uses in preventing planning or market blight arising from vacant sites should be apparent to all.

This chapter has therefore suggested a range of ways in which existing low-value land uses, that play an important role for communities can be protected and also created, provided the planning system is able to recognise their significance.

NINE

Assets in common

This chapter looks at assets that are used in common by local communities. These include open spaces used for leisure and/or contributing to the amenity of an area. They also include buildings that can host a variety of activities that meet a community's needs. These common assets can be important sources of support to communities, providing them with resources and benefits that they cannot otherwise find, either within their own homes or outside. If a family does not have a garden, then the local park is vital as somewhere to take the children to play. If membership of the private health club is too expensive, classes run at the community centre can support the health of local people. If an elderly single person finds it too expensive to go to a local cafe, then the coffee mornings held at the local church can provide a reason to get out and meet people. While higher-income households can afford to use the facilities that the market provides – at a price – to enhance their quality of life, these assets in the public realm are of vital significance to those who cannot.[1] Similarly, higher-income households can afford to travel to localities where a wider range of services and amenities are available. Lower-income households are more dependent on what is offered by the immediate locality.

As Flint says:[2]

> All neighbourhoods require a minimum standard of retail, service and housing infrastructure. This requires a combination of public policy and investment and contributions from the voluntary, community and private sectors. The vagaries of private sector investment will not deliver sustainability in lower income urban neighbourhoods.

So how can the planning system ensure the local public realm supports the needs of the local community, including the more vulnerable sectors within that community?

The limitations of private provision and management

At one time, the simple answer to ensuring that the public realm offered a range of communal facilities was direct provision by the public sector, often the local authority. This would extend both to services such as leisure services – the swimming pool, the bowling green, the tennis courts – as well as the provision and management of public spaces, both parks and urban squares and other spaces in the public realm. However, the funds available to local government to support the public realm in this way have been under constraint for several decades now, for a mix of economic and ideological reasons.

This has put the emphasis onto engagement with the private sector to underpin this provision, but relying on the market to supply these needs directly is unlikely to meet all the community's needs for two reasons. First, markets respond to demand not need, and will only meet needs in so far as there is a 'willingness to pay', including, of course, an ability to pay. Those with available funds and a desire to spend them on specific facilities will probably find the private sector responding; others will not. In itself this need not be problematic – few societies are able to meet all their citizens' desires and there seems little moral case for doing so.

However, this is problematic where either there are important needs (not just wants) that are going unmet, or where there is a broader public interest that is undermined by this under-supply of key aspects of the public realm. For example, health can be considered a basic human right, and access to an environment that promotes exercise through active mobility for leisure or utilitarian purposes can be a key element in promoting such health. In addition, given the costs of the health service to the public purse, it can be argued that there is a public as well as individual interest in promoting better health in this way. The Government Office for Science has puts the costs to the NHS of overweight and obesity at £5 billion per annum, and the wider costs to society and business as rising to almost £50 billion per annum by 2050.[3] Relying on the market to provide community facilities and a quality of local environment that promotes health will not result in all citizens having equal or even adequate access to these facilities and environmental resources; those with funds to spend and a desire to spend them will be prioritised. Private tennis clubs will be supplied; facilities for lower-income households to practise their preferred leisure activities will not.

Second, the market favours the provision of services and goods that are 'private', where people other than the owner can be excluded from their enjoyment. This is because others will have to pay if they also wish to enjoy it. Where there is the possibility of free-riding – of someone enjoying a good or service that someone else has paid for – then the market is likely to undersupply that good or service. This is particularly the case with many facilities and services in the public realm. A local park or open space is likely to be available to all who wish to use it, at least in daylight hours. Entry to such spaces is rarely charged for. Therefore the market has little incentive to provide such spaces. Where access can be restricted, then the market may react differently. In London, access to the green space in the middle of certain urban squares established in the 18th centuries is restricted to keyholders of the surrounding properties. The cost of supplying that space is captured in the enhanced value of the surrounding property, and the market has an incentive to build such open spaces into urban developments. However, apart from the visual amenity, such squares are not truly in the public realm. Gated communities are extending this trend.[4]

As previous chapters have emphasised, the central premise of growth-dependent planning is that, during the regulation process through which development permission is granted, part of the development profits will be directed towards providing some form of community benefit, including certain community facilities or improvements to aspects of the urban realm. In addition to the problem that has been highlighted throughout the preceding discussion – of the dependence of these benefits on urban development being sufficiently profitable – there are additional concerns relating to the onward management and hence accessibility of the facilities and public space delivered through these means.

The issue here is that such benefits require ongoing management. It is not enough just to fund a community centre or leisure facility or nature reserve or new public square through the mechanism of planning gain. All of these aspects of the public realm require ongoing management to ensure that they continue to fulfil their functions. This in itself has financial implications. If money is to be set aside for ongoing management from the development profits – in the form of some kind of fund – then this will increase the share expected from development profits, and make the negotiation even more dependent on the profitability of the development. If management funds are not to be negotiated in this way, this raises the question of where they will come from and who will bear the burden of continuing to maintain and manage this community asset.

For example, the capital costs of providing a public park may be provided from planning gain, but without ongoing maintenance this will become more of a community liability than an asset. The developer may pay a lump sum to provide for future management, but this raises the costs of the planning gain, which is ultimately limited by the economic viability of the development, and it is further doubtful if such sums provide for the full costs of such management over time.

In addition to the financial aspects of management and maintenance, there are important issues regarding accessibility. Who will the community asset continue to be managed for? If these decisions are left in private sector hands, then it may be that the asset will not be made available to those most in need of it. Access may be restricted as the asset becomes subject to market criteria. The fact that the original investment in the asset was a result of a planning gain negotiation may be lost as it essentially reverts to a private sector management regime.

Minton has emphasised the recent trend towards privatisation of urban spaces, particularly where these are provided as planning gain associated with new developments.[5] There has been a tendency, as part of the urban design renaissance, to expect new urban developments of any size to make a positive contribution to the public realm through landscaping and provision of urban spaces that are available to the public to enjoy. However, these spaces remain in private ownership and are thus public in a more limited sense than many may expect. There are specific concerns in Scotland where some land has a different legal status as common good land. In both Aberdeen and Edinburgh cases have been reported of such common good land being given over to private developers under long leases.[6]

It could be argued that ownership is less important than management and that, provided access to the general public is ensured, the private ownership of the sites – often unified with the ownership of the surrounding development – merely provides a means whereby the ongoing management of the space is guaranteed. Given that part of the purpose of the open space is to provide a setting to the new development that enhances its value, it can be argued that such ongoing management is more likely to preserve the qualities of the open space, to the benefit also of the general public. The problem arises if, as a result of this private ownership and because of the private management of the space, access becomes restricted either at certain times of day or to certain groups. In some cases, the 'public' space can become a gated space during the evening or night. Or the private management of a space that is still in private ownership may result in certain groups – say, young people – being excluded on the grounds that they are not engaged in the activities that the owners envisage as suitable for the site.[7]

This suggests that there are dangers inherent in the private ownership and management of community facilities and public spaces. But in the absence of sufficient public funds to take such assets into public ownership and management, what are the alternatives? The following discussion considers how community ownership and management itself may provide an appropriate pathway, ensuring such assets are provided and are accessible to all, particularly lower-income households, meeting their specific needs.

Community ownership and management

There are multiple examples in existence of community management and ownership of assets that are an integral part of the everyday lives of local people.[8] Research by the Joseph Rowntree Foundation emphasised that there is a history of such community involvement dating back over 400 years.[9] The key feature of such involvement is its variety. Religious institutions often use their property to support community activities, with some churches and temples acting as community centres for their localities. Childcare, afterschool homework clubs, elder care including lunchtime clubs, food banks and daily canteens are all widespread. But many other community-based activities can be found that are not based in particular religious affiliations.

Numerous community groups engage in the management of their local parks and nature reserves through organisations such as local wildlife trusts or 'Friends of...' groups. Indeed the Royal Society for the Protection of Birds (RSPB) relies on such groups to carry much of the burden for the daily oversight of their reserves.[10] Such groups organise on a regular basis to undertaken periodic clean-ups and also act as watchdogs for any more serious threat or problem with the open spaces. These groups are not only offering their time and attention, but also often considerable expertise with regard to horticulture, biodiversity and conservation.

Allotments for food growing can also be run under community rather than local authority management, such as those in Todmorden, West Yorkshire.[11] The community orchard movement also falls within this category. In Crouch End, London, a site left over after the development of a new health centre was leased to a local community group as a community orchard. As it abuts onto a secondary school, there are now plans to build an outdoor classroom there out of straw bales to provide education opportunities for local young adults and children. The House of Commons Environmental Audit Committee, however, has criticised the NPPF for providing insufficient guidance on how to support these community-based food growing initiatives.[12]

Given the importance of shops to supporting everyday life, community retail facilities are particularly important. Not only do they provide local services for those who find it difficult to travel any distance because they do not have access to cheap, accessible and convenient transport; they can also act as a social hub and thus provide essential social contact, building local networks of friendships and acquaintances that are essential for human well-being and resilience in times of trouble.

In *The purpose of planning*, the case of Blockley village shop was highlighted, a community facility that now houses a post office, a cafe with internet connection and a nursery as well as everyday goods for sale.[13] An example that has been repeatedly highlighted in the press is the People's Supermarket near Holborn, London. Set up by Arthur Potts Dawson in 2010, this is run as a cooperative with local people having an ownership share but also working in the shop. It now has a turnover of nearly £1.3 million per annum and has created 17 full and part-time jobs. However, the financial robustness of its business model has been questioned by the decision to go into partnership with Spar, raising £100,000 to secure its future.[14] Other examples include the Real Food Store in Exeter that sells locally grown vegetables, has a bakery and also runs a cafe within the store, and the Unicorn Grocery in Manchester which is branching out into local food production as well as retailing. Many of these are constituted as Community Benefit Societies or BenComs which require that the operation is to the benefit of the wider community.

Public houses have also been taken into community ownership given their importance as a local meeting point, particularly in rural areas. The Butchers Arms in Crosby Ravensworth, Cumbria, which opened under such ownership in August 2011, and the Golden Ball in York are two such examples. Altogether it was estimated in May 2012 that there were some 300 community-run shops and nine community-run pubs operating in the UK. The government now have a Community Pubs Minister and have provided (rather minimal) financial support to the Pub is the Hub organisation.[15]

Other community buildings can also be used as multi-use centres. In Cambridgeshire, the community college concept involved the buildings that housed a secondary school during the day being used for a range of community uses, including over the weekend and in the evenings. For example, Cottenham Community College has run a bank out of the school which provided a local service and also gave work experience to students. This kind of activity can be threatened by security concerns, however, necessitating strong local community networks of trust to make it work. Where schools have been provided on a Private Finance Initiative, this kind of flexible use can be more difficult as the ownership rests with a private body which is primarily concerned with providing the contracted service and receiving a viable asset back at the end of the contract.

Libraries are another potentially important community asset. Beyond lending books, music and DVDs, they can provide space for community meetings, art exhibitions (including, say, from local schools), study space, book clubs, cafes and even night-time cinema screenings. Local authority financial cutbacks are seeing some libraries now being taken over by community groups, which may result in these community-based activities being expanded. For example, in London, a number of individual libraries threatened with closure by their host borough council are now being run by community-based groups using volunteers.[16] On a larger scale, on 1 August 2012 Suffolk County Council passed its entire libraries service of 44 libraries over to an Industrial and Provident Society which will work in partnership with a variety of local community organisations.[17] These transfers are controversial since it is unclear where the ongoing financial support for book purchases and building maintenance will come from, in addition to the potential loss of professional expertise from librarians – volunteer labour and fees for use of the buildings can only go so far. The Suffolk case has also raised issues of transparency and accountability in relation to the statutory responsibility that the council still hold for ensuring a county-wide library network.

Overall, the Joseph Rowntree Foundation research has identified three overlapping but largely different approaches to such community engagement with assets:[18]

- **stewards** tend to be small, volunteer-based and focused on a single long-standing asset such as a building;
- **community developers** are more medium-sized organisations with a range of assets and an involvement in local service delivery and wider partnerships, often with hired staff and a mix of income sources; and
- **entrepreneurs** are the largest examples, often run as professional social enterprises and with a mix of capital-intensive assets for social and commercial uses.

The key message is that there is potential for fitting community management to a variety of local circumstances, needs and community resources, although some services and functions may go beyond the capacities of even the larger community organisations.

The support of such community-based ownership and management has been particularly emphasised under the 2011 Localism Act and the associated Coalition government agenda for a 'Big Society', but the New Labour government also put in place measures to encourage such community involvement. The 2006 Local Government White Paper, the 2007 Local Government and Public Involvement in Health Act and the 2008 Community Empowerment White Paper all included such measures. The Quirk Review of community management and ownership of public assets argued for the mainstreaming of this approach, and led to the Asset Transfer Unit being set up; since 2009 this has been delivered by the NGO Locality along with the Local Government Association.[19]

In the devolved regimes, there has been similar action. In Wales the 2005 Assembly Strategy on social enterprise set specific targets for contracts, asset transfer and asset refurbishment for social enterprises, while in Northern Ireland a Community Support Programme in 2007 specifically targeted community centres. Scotland has, however, been particularly pro-active with legislation giving communities the right to buy. The 2003 Land Reform (Scotland) Act has enabled significant community land buy-outs in Scotland, particularly in the Western Isles.

Buying and funding community assets

The Joseph Rowntree Foundation research makes it clear that community involvement of these kinds takes different forms in different countries. In the UK the ownership of the asset plays a particularly important role. The Development Trust Association estimated in 2010 that its member organisations held £520 million-worth of assets.[20]

The 2011 Localism Act introduced a Community Right to Bid (CRB) for community assets following the example set by Scotland. The CRB works by creating a 'list of assets of community value' and community organisations and parish councils nominating assets in their locality for inclusion. Assets stay on the list for a period of five years. The criteria for deciding an asset is of 'community value' are broadly that the use of the land or building currently, or in the recent past, furthers the 'social well-being or social interests of the local community' and that this use will continue to do so. The kinds of interests that are particularly mentioned relate to cultural, recreational and sporting uses. This use must also be the principle use of the land or buildings, not an ancillary one. Derelict sites are unlikely to come within the compass of the CRB.[21]

If the owner of any nominated assets wishes to sell, there is a moratorium period during which a sale cannot proceed. There is an initial six-week period for the community group to notify that they are a potential bidder, and then a full six-month period which gives community groups time to try and raise the finances to bid for the asset when it is put up for sale at the end of that period. The community group has no right to buy – the CRB just gives them time to try and be in a position to buy. The price is set by open market trading; there is no discount for community groups. There are some exemptions, including disposal by gift or within a family and where the land or building is part of a larger estate or part of a going concern and continuing business.

It is clear that community groups rather than local authorities are the key actors here, but local planners can also play a supporting role. The NGO Locality suggests that this role can encompass:[22]

- the mapping of assets in a locality;
- building a shared understanding of a community's needs, ambitions and capacities;
- being transparent about the potential need to dispose of surplus public sector assets to reduce conflict with community projects;
- considering the sustainability implications of developing these assets; and
- stimulating creative ideas about how services could be delivered and where they should be based.

However, the limitation of the CRB is that sales are still made in the open market and at full market value, unless the seller is willing to accept a price below this full market value. However, if this were the case, it would probably not be necessary to invoke the CRB in the first place. There is, though, the potential for public sector assets to be transferred to the community at 'less than best consideration'. This is termed a Community Asset Transfer and is one way to get around the general provision that public sector land and buildings have to be sold for their highest economic value. For a Community Asset Transfer to work, the land or buildings must be intended to further local social, economic and/or environmental objectives and be to a community organisation.

Clearly a fundamental requirement for community assets to play these creative roles in providing for local communities' needs is some finance, both for running costs and management, but also, if ownership is to underpin such management and to offer greater control, for buying an equity stake in the asset. Whether full market value or a discounted value for a community asset is involved, community groups will have to raise funding for buying assets. Internal resources within the community are likely to be limited, particularly in lower-income communities, so that recourse will have to be made to grants and loans.

There have been dedicated central government funding streams for asset transfer to local communities. These include the Adventure Capital Fund, Futurebuilders and the Community Assets Fund. As part of the Big Society agenda, the current Coalition government have arranged for £400 million from dormant bank accounts to be used to finance Big Society Capital, with a further donation of £200 million from the four big banks, Barclays, Lloyds, HSBC and RBS. One other possibility that could be explored is the greater use of the CIL charged on new developments to support such community initiatives. However, this is assuming that there is sufficient new development occurring in a locality to provide such finances, and remains very much within the growth-dependent approach to skimming off resources for social benefit from the promotion of private sector development.

Other sources of finance are likely to come from more creative forms of lending. In particular, loans that can be built up from many smaller donations seem applicable to financing such community projects. Crowdfunding is an interesting development here. The Real Food Store in Exeter, mentioned earlier, raised funds by selling £153,000 in community shares to 287 investors. The Manchester Unicorn Grocery bought its 21 acres for local food production partly with loans from its own customers, who could choose an interest rate of between 0 and 4 per cent on their loan. Cultivate Oxford, a food delivery BenCom, raised £80,000 from 200 investors within the community. Bigton Community Shop funded itself by creating a share issue attracting over 100 local members.

The possibility of income streams from generating renewable energy on a community scale is giving rise to a range of new initiatives focused around energy.[23] For example, one interesting example is Woolhope Heat. This claims to be the country's first wood fuel cooperative. It raised funds from a range of investors with a minimum stake of £250. It installs biomass CHP boilers in local premises in Herefordshire, retaining ownership and committing to ongoing maintenance. It then supplies these boilers with local woodchip, making money by selling the heat generated. It also benefits currently from the Renewable Heat Incentive. Given the range of government grants available for renewable energy generation, these kinds of community enterprises are able to blend government support with community fundraising and provide a sustainable local service. They are, however, vulnerable to changes in grant regimes, and these have proved particularly unstable during the recent period of public sector cutbacks. Other examples are the Brighton and Bristol Energy cooperatives.[24]

Crowdfunding is the ultimate extension of such financing, using the web to bring in multiple small donations to support new ideas. This was originally used to help creative start-ups and art projects through sites such as Kickstarter, Indiegogo and ArtistShare, but has now moved into built environment projects or crowdfunded urbanism. In the US, CivicSponsor, and in Finland, Brickstarter, are sites devoted to this; Spacehive is the UK equivalent.[25] They have supported a range of projects, from a forest garden in Stockwell,

London, to a community centre in Pontypridd, Wales. All projects on the site have a fixed financial target and money is only taken from donors if this target is met. The benefits to the donors are clearly stated. Spacehive get a management fee to provide the projects with a sustainable financial basis. For this they have an advisory board to undertake due diligence on all projects prior to fundraising. They also offer technical advice through onsite tools and volunteer professionals. Once the funds are raised, the project delivery manager is contractually obliged to undertake and finish the project.

As well as specific one-off projects, such funding is underpinning the creation of social enterprises that are developing community-based plans for transforming neighbourhoods. Two examples are Stokes Croft in Bristol and the Gasworks Dock Partnership in Newham, London.[26] In Stokes Croft an explicitly radical perspective is being taken on neighbourhood planning; as their website states:

> The area has pioneered a liberal attitude towards street art, and is working towards an alternative to conventional top-down government. Liberal attitudes have led to a blossoming of positive energy as this part of the City, neglected and abused by planners and local government, forges its own future, resisting conventional gentrification and the pressures of developers and corporate business, safeguarding its unique identity against the blandification threatened by conventional development.

The Newham project is perhaps more conventional in tone. It seeks to provide a framework for community-led regeneration based around the revitalisation of local waterways. One initiative is the Docklands community boat based at Cody Dock, a 2.5 acre site that will be used as the location for a range of other social enterprises and community activities.

Other innovative sources of finance are also being discussed. For example, ResPublica, in association with the Royal Institute of British Architects, has proposed a range of measures including the issue of specific forms of paper debt such as Social Impact Bonds and Social Investment Bonds.[27] The current form of Real Estate Investment

Trusts – which enable the securitisation of property investment so that multiple small equity stakes are possible rather than one single lump investment by ownership – could be restructured to support community ownership. They term this a 'Community Right to Invest in Real Estate'.

Managing community assets

Once the asset has been identified, funded and bought, the work of running it on a sustainable basis for community benefit follows. It might seem a long way from the plains of Africa to the problems of towns and cities in the UK, but the debate about how these grazing lands get degraded and could be better protected provides some interesting ideas about how community assets can be managed. The two key issues are how an asset used in common can be viable enough to be supplied, and how use of that asset can be managed to avoid it being over-exploited. Before exploring these issues in relation to urban community assets, the debate about those African plains is briefly related below.

This debate refers to the so-called 'tragedy of the commons'. The original argument – expounded by Garrett Hardin – ran like this.[28] There is a group of tribesmen whose main livelihood comes from the cattle that they raise. The cattle are individually owned but the grazing land for these cattle is held in common and is open-access so that anyone who wants to can use the land. Each individual herder sees no reason not to add more cattle to the grazing land; on the contrary, there is a clear advantage for them to use as much of the pasture as possible. However, beyond a certain point, the pasture will not support the number of cattle, and the grazing will become degraded. Yet, individual grazers will continue to add more cattle to the grazing herd if they possibly can, as their cattle will still be getting some benefit from the pasture. The problem here is a divergence between the individual calculus of each herdsman who sees a personal benefit in putting another cow or bull onto the pasture, and the collective calculus of the whole group who would benefit from the pasture being managed so as to maintain the quality of its grazing and prevent it being turned into a dustbowl.

This 'tragedy of the commons' argument has been used to explain many different forms of environmental pollution and degradation: climate change, air pollution, over-fishing, excessive water abstraction, landscape erosion. And it has also been used to promote the benefits of market solutions to such problems.[29] The advocates of these market solutions argue that since the root cause of the problem is the ownership of land in common, the answer is to split up and privatise the land so that each herdsman has his own patch of grazing. By extension, this would involve privatising all sorts of environmental assets to ensure their protection.

But quite a different lesson can be taken from Hardin's parable, and this is a lesson that has been supported by considerable research (notably by Elinor Ostrom) on how such common assets are actually used.[30] This has identified that the problem lies not in the common ownership but in the nature of the management regime that the group has agreed on. In Hardin's parable, there is no management regime – it is a free for all. Ostrom has shown that in many cases of such common pool resources, held in common, the group is a defined one and has developed sets of rules for agreeing how the resource should be used: when, by whom and for how long or how much. They also importantly have arrangements in place for resolving any conflicts. In this way many resources held in common are managed sustainably, yielding benefits for all the individuals involved and also ensuring the collective group has access to this resource into the future.

What has been created through these management regimes are institutions of genuinely common ownership, or common property regimes. This is in contrast to the Hardin parable where the nature of the open access meant that no one actually owned the pastures. Ownership by an individual, a company or a group always implies a set of rules governing use, and ownership in common is no exception. So the key lesson that this debate has for community assets everywhere is the importance of community engagement with and commitment to a management regime for the asset, to manage its use and to ensure its sustainability.

This is partly about crafting institutional arrangements such as the legal documents setting up a trust or society so that there is transparency about how management decisions will be made and conflicts resolved. But research has also emphasised the importance of relationships within the local community. The key concept here is social capital. This refers to the density of connections between members of a group – here, the 'local community' – and also the way that these relationships are imbued with norms of trust, reciprocity and mutuality. The idea is that social capital will be present to a greater degree in a locality where a large number of people know each other and know each other well, where they trust each other and will do things for each in other in the name of a commonly held joint enterprise. Such social capital will then enable common management of jointly held assets.

This might seem self-evident and sensible, but the concept of social capital is a little more complex than this suggests.[31] Theorists have distinguished different kinds of social capital, notably the difference between bonding and bridging social capital. Bonding social capital acts as a form of strong glue and is evident through very close ties between community members. It ties together community members who are alike in some respect, creating a more homogeneous group. Bridging social capital is a looser form of linkage and is generally considered a way of tying people who are rather different together.

This account immediately raises the issue of how people relate to each other and what they consider they have in common. This is at the heart of what can be considered to constitute a 'community'. The term is often used as if it is self-evident as to what comprises a community, as if there has been a process of spatial sorting whereby similar people live next to each other. This is certainly no longer the case, if it ever has been. Thus the above discussion has often referred to communities in the plural. People today have multiple allegiances, multiple relationships of different kinds and many different facets to their identity. The nature of the ties within a group of people who happen to live (and perhaps work) in a defined neighbourhood or spatial area can be complex to map.

Defining any particular community will include some people and provide a basis for their common interests, but it will exclude others. Social capital and communities are both concepts that emphasise boundaries as much as inclusion. Thus the group of people who develop links around a local school will be quite different from a group developing around a religious building. Both will be inclusive, in relation to people with children in the first case and people who are members of a particular faith in the latter. But they are also likely to be exclusive for many of the activities that these community assets run. Child safety concerns will limit access to school-based activities and a high level of trust is needed for sharing childcare itself. Religious institutions may open up their doors to people from the locality more generally, but many may not wish to be involved with such institutions or dislike the basis – say, a charitable basis – on which they are being invited in.

This puts the emphasis on building many different forms of social capital within a specific spatial area if community-based ownership and management of common assets is to be successful. It is also about enabling more bridging social capital to be created; both the school and religious institution examples are cases where strong bonding social capital is being built. This is about inclusion and relationships between people who may not see themselves as having much in common. Some community assets are by definition more inclusive. Everyone can use a village shop or a library or a post office without considering whether they are part of 'the group' or not.

The discussion so far has emphasised issues of community development through social capital and also the creation of management regimes for regulating that community involvement. But what can planning specifically do to contribute to the successful community management of local assets?

There is a role involved in identifying assets that may be of value to local groups within the locality. This task can be a specific part of local planning exercises. Planning can also use its regulatory powers to protect such assets from threats of development, although this raises questions about the current nature of development control and whether it is fine-grained enough, a point already returned to in Chapter 10. But probably the most important role that planning can play is in terms of creating a sense of a local community that goes beyond a set of self-defined and quite tightly bounded groups. It can identify the 'community' in an inclusive way and work to bring together different groups, creating the bridging social capital that will be essential for the effective management of assets for all local residents and occupiers.

Gallent and Robinson have identified how the real benefit of community and neighbourhood planning has been to galvanise local people into thinking about their locality from the perspective of all local users.[32] They highlight the dangers of needing to rely on a few leaders in this process, and the inevitably small number of activists who get engaged in such activities. But it does seem that the very act of developing a local strategy for a neighbourhood, one which includes an explicit role for a number of community assets, can help to bring together a community and build the types of social capital that are necessary for successful, inclusive and sustainable management of those assets.

TEN

Reforming the planning system

The argument of the book

There is a wealth of literature on planning that has identified weaknesses, limitations and areas for reform. The critical nature of planning research ensures this. The inability of the system to deal with social inequality and environmental injustice has been repeatedly commented on, and this book is another contribution to this ongoing debate. However, the last three chapters have pointed to a wide range of initiatives that are already happening and that suggest a different way forward, as well as avenues for further reform. Together they may constitute a more resilient form of planning in situations of economic downturn and low growth, and may also offer possibilities to low-income communities for improving their quality of life and developing more environmentally sustainable localities, possibilities that are not delivered on by growth-dependent planning. They could, therefore, underpin a revised planning agenda for just sustainability. But to be effective they require a different structure of policy guidance and a new set of planning tools. The role of community engagement also needs to be rethought and widened. The purpose of this chapter is to flesh out some key elements of this different paradigm.

In offering this revised approach, it is important to emphasise that these reforms are not intended to completely displace the growth-dependent planning that has been critiqued in this book. Hopefully it has been demonstrated that growth dependence has significant flaws, particularly as a way of ensuring that all groups in society have equal access to an environment that meets their needs, provides a good quality of life and contributes to sustainability. This is the case even when the underlying economic conditions for growth-dependent planning are present; some groups always get left behind or are displaced by the outcomes. But in conditions of low economic growth – nationally, regionally or locally – it is even more important to develop a different approach that is not reliant on growth to deliver benefits.

However, this does not mean that growth-dependent planning has no place at all within the planning system. There will be times and places where considerable social benefits and environmental protection or enhancement can be generated from facilitating private sector development and using a share of development profits to meet a variety of goals. Care needs to be taken to ensure that any promises for broader social welfare and environmental sustainability are actually met. But in a society where the private sector controls the main monetary means of investment in urban and environmental change, growth-dependent planning does offer a means of using that investment to achieve more than private benefit.

The argument of this book is that a reliance on growth-dependent planning *alone* is insufficient. It is insufficient to meet the needs of all sectors of society, to ensure quality of life for all households and a more sustainable future. It is not addressing major social inequalities, including environmental injustices. It is not always supporting the well-being agenda so as to challenge the dominance of the pursuit of economic growth. It is not enabling natural resources and ecosystem services to be sufficiently stewarded, promoting continued exploitation even where claims are made for green growth. Therefore this final chapter is about rebalancing the planning system towards just sustainability rather than replacing growth-based planning with another paradigm. It sets out the reforms that need to be incorporated into the planning system *alongside* the effective use of growth-based planning to deliver on public benefits.

This chapter therefore outlines the way that plans, regulation and other planning tools – particularly landownership and fiscal measures – and community engagement can operate beyond the growth-dependent paradigm.

Reformed planning policy guidance

The importance of central government policy guidance was emphasised in Chapter 2. Such central government policy guidance carries considerable force due to the principle of conformity of plans, with plans and policies formulated at a higher government tier. This is reinforced by the way that planning regulation operates, particularly through the planning appeal system. At present the NPPF, as the current expression of central government planning policy, ensures that growth-dependent planning dominates.[1] However, there is scope for incorporating a different approach through reforms to such guidance. Chapters 7 to 9 have identified a range of specific proposals but, to set the context for these, it is necessary to ensure that the core objectives and values of the reformed planning agenda proposed in Chapter 6 are also incorporated.

Thus it is proposed that the NPPF should be amended to reflect the central principles, not only of well-being (which is already given emphasis) and sustainability (which is referenced), but also of tackling inequalities and environmental injustice. In effect the NPPF should reflect the need to promote just sustainability. The experience with environmental justice in the US provides some guidance for this. Under the Clinton administration, the Environmental Protection Agency (EPA) was charged with taking environmental justice into account in its decision making. It now operates with a working definition of environmental justice as:[2]

> Environmental Justice is the fair treatment and meaningful involvement of all people regardless of race, color, national origin, or income with respect to the development, implementation, and enforcement of environmental laws, regulations, and policies. EPA has this goal for all communities and persons across this Nation. It will be achieved when everyone enjoys the same degree of protection from environmental and health hazards and equal access to the decision-making process to have a healthy environment in which to live, learn, and work.

There is also some support for this within the European policy framework. The Aarhus Convention seeks to embed environmental justice within environmental policy making and decision making.[3] However, it has taken a largely procedural route so that justice is linked to certain rights that public authorities are required to make effective:

- the right to receive environmental information;
- the right to participate in environmental decision making; and
- the right to review procedures to challenge public decisions with respect to the operationalisation of the first two rights.

This procedural approach to incorporating environmental justice concerns is much less effective than the substantive approach adopted by the US EPA in terms of ensuring that vulnerable communities are protected and able to shape their local environments in pursuit of well-being and sustainability. Incorporating a commitment to substantive environmental justice (preferably framed as just sustainability) within central government policy guidance would give a significant resource to vulnerable communities to influence plans and planning decisions.

Beyond this fundamental reform, the discussions in Chapters 7 to 9 have suggested a number of policies that should be embedded in local plans in order to support planning for well-being and just sustainability; they also require support within central government guidance. Incorporating such guidance in the NPPF would both encourage local authorities to adopt a 'beyond growth dependence' approach and also give support to those policies in local and neighbourhood plans. The reforms proposed are:

- support for exceptions policies where planning permission can be exceptionally given provided that it can be demonstrated that the development would meet the needs, particularly housing needs, of lower-income communities;
- allocation of sites specifically for community-based development, such as through CLTs or self-build;

- more emphasis on policies for higher-density development and mixed-use developments where these can create low-value premises;
- support for area improvement plans for both residential and town centre areas with particular emphasis on improved energy efficiency and other features that improve well-being and environmental sustainability but are less valued by market demand;
- recognition of the importance of secondary and tertiary shopping areas, SME spaces and markets;
- recognition of the value of temporary uses and the need to make use of vacant land and property;
- policies supporting meanwhile uses and the flexible application of planning regulation in such cases; and
- support for the changes to planning regulation that are proposed below.

The purpose of these changes is to incorporate, at the highest policy level, an explicit recognition that land uses – bare sites or buildings – with a low market value can still be important in meeting community needs. Such recognition would then balance the more numerous references to the need for planning to support and promote development that increases land and property values. It would mean that terminology such as the 'vitality' of shopping centres would need to be adjusted to incorporate the aim of providing lower-priced shopping opportunities as well as promoting the location of multiples and increasing retail expenditure in total. 'Competitiveness' would not be the sole metaphor for town centre management, offering a place for secondary and tertiary land uses within the vision of a 'vital' town centre. Where the current NPPF suggests (p 8) that 'where town centres are in decline, local planning authorities should plan positively for their future to encourage economic activity', reference should instead be made to the importance of 'meeting community retail needs'. This is not the place for a detailed redrafting; rather, the point is the importance of ensuring that central government makes full reference to, and hence supports planning beyond growth dependence, where that is the more desirable approach.

Reformed planning tools

The planning tool box is currently rather limited and the tools available are not well suited to promoting planning beyond growth dependence. In particular, planning regulation needs to be recast to be much more effective in protecting the land and assets that currently contribute to just sustainability through meeting the needs of lower-income communities. It also needs to be more capable of positively promoting development and land uses that also contribute to the just sustainability agenda. In addition, the planning tool box needs to use the powers of landownership to a greater extent and alongside certain fiscal measures.

So considering the reform of planning regulation, the discussion in the preceding chapters has emphasised the importance of regulation in a variety of ways. Planning regulation is essential for protecting certain existing land uses, determining which kinds of development can go forward and negotiating planning gain. It also, in conjunction with market processes, contributes to the structuring of local land markets. A variety of ways of reforming regulation have been suggested:

- firm application of the application of land allocation policies where market-led development is concerned to avoid speculative planning applications and the creation of hope value in land markets;
- implementation of exceptions policies as a means of releasing land for community-based development at existing use value;
- release of sites for community-based options such as self-build;
- flexibility with regard to the application of standard development control requirements for options such as eco-build that contribute to just sustainability;
- designation of community assets supporting justice and sustainability (or some other better nomenclature) to protect certain land uses that are of use value to communities and promote equality and environmental sustainability;
- linking planning consents with specific classes of occupier by specifying classes of occupier in individual planning consents and potentially supporting this with area-based policies;

- using policies that specify certain scales of development and land use to protect small-scale land uses from amalgamation on (re-) development;
- policies to permit pop-up land uses and applying flexibility in regulating such cases;
- flexibility in development control for meanwhile uses;
- requiring provision for meanwhile uses in case of development being delayed through planning conditions attached to development consents; and
- relaxation of the strict application of precedent in regulatory decision making where the test of contributing to well-being and just sustainability can be applied.

This book is focused on the planning system, but it should be recognised that such reforms of planning regulation should go alongside the firm implementation of regulations for adequate housing standards and environmental protection that exist within other governmental regimes. Regulation of the built environment needs to be able to ensure basic minimum standards of environmental health are achieved. Why should it be possible routinely to rent out housing that is damp, mouldy and hard to heat? Similarly, regulation of sources of pollution is clearly a priority, both with regard to point sources such as industrial complexes but also the diffuse pollution associated with road-based transport. As well as regulation of the technologies of transport, the Greater London Authority have shown how zoning systems can be used to control traffic in an area (although with the risk of simply moving the traffic and associated pollution elsewhere), and to influence the adoption of cleaner technology within vehicles.[4]

But regulation is not the only planning tool that is needed to move beyond growth dependence. The above discussion has identified two other important tools: use of landownership rights and financial instruments including subsidies and taxation.

One point that has been repeatedly returned to is the potential for meshing the planners' role in drawing up local plans with the power of local authority landownership. If local authorities were able to use their own land to guide where development should go, this would overcome a key weakness in current planning. This is how the more effective planning regimes in cities such as Stockholm, Malmö and Freiburg have operated. Using public landownership also allows the local authority to impose requirements on the subsequent development that are additional to identifying the desired land use. However, the UK planning system has had an unhappy history of attempts to base local planning on public sector landownership. This is partly because these attempts have focused on programmes of land nationalisation rather than building up local authority landbanks incrementally over time. It is also partly because of an ideological opposition to local authority landownership by successive governments (usually, but not always, Conservative governments) and a tendency to use sales of public sector land as a way to raise public finance.

In this context, the following reforms regarding landownership should be considered:

- transferring public land to communities at existing use value;
- using and enabling community land ownership structures;
- using local authority powers to take over empty homes on a temporary or permanent basis;
- using specific mortgages to transfer empty homes and other properties to local residents and community groups; and
- using and enabling meanwhile leases.

In addition to transferring land and property rights, there is a need for financial resources to fulfil some of the elements discussed in Chapters 7 to 9. On fiscal measures there is a need for:

- providing funding for the purchase of land for community development and assets for community management;
- considering innovative ways to raise such finances;
- funding the re-use of empty homes, through both subsidies for necessary works and loans to enable their ownership to be transferred;
- extending subsidies for energy efficiency measures for those in fuel poverty;

- reinstating grants for area improvement under community guidance for existing residential and SME needs; and
- considering changes to tax and grant regimes to incentivise the re-use of empty property, such as the removal of VAT on refurbishment; this may require specific investigation to identify how the complexities of current fiscal measures are acting as a barrier to such re-use.

Reformed community engagement

It should be clear from this that the policies, plans and regulatory frameworks of the planning system could support community activities and needs to a greater extent. Landownership powers, community funding and investment in residential areas and town centres could then support the capacities of local communities, particularly lower-income communities, to shape their localities to meet their needs. This does imply a different form of community engagement, however, beyond the procedural approach to consultation or even collaborative discussions during development proposals and plan making. This is more about creating social capital within residential and local business communities to enable action for community-based initiatives. It is about community building, using the resources of connectivity, trust, mutuality and reciprocity that already exist within and between groups co-living in an area.

Gallent and Robinson have pointed to how the processes of community planning and neighbourhood planning, although often frustrating to communities in terms of getting the control of new development that they aspire to, have helped to bond communities and generate the social capital that is at the heart of community building.[5] North American planners also have much experience of community development to offer UK planning practice. But this would go beyond the rather formal, procedural framing of planning activity that the UK planning system offers.

The tentative steps towards neighbourhood planning offer the prospects for change here, although they require local planners to engage with specific communities in much more depth and over a longer time span than before. In effect this suggests a shift from communities engaging with planning processes to planners engaging with community dynamics and understanding what makes the community work, including the internal differences, tensions, cleavages and conflicts. This will require substantial resources (additional or diverted) in terms of personnel and also training, the development of specialist expertise and learning from grass-roots experiences that is already happening, often overseas. There is a wealth of guidance material available that can be drawn on.[6]

The challenge is to reorient at least part of the planning system towards prioritising such planner–community engagement. To this end the following reforms to community engagement practices are proposed:

- ensuring that all community engagement provides full, supported opportunities for the voices of lower-income and vulnerable communities to be heard, alongside those representing the just sustainability agenda;
- understanding, utilising and supporting existing social capital to enable community-based development projects;
- utilising existing social capital for the management of community assets, providing support through appropriate management structures for collective decision making and conflict resolution; and
- using social capital that exists specifically within local business communities to support town centre enhancement.

Bringing it all together

This chapter has brought together analysis made throughout the book into a programme for reform. The new mode of planning is summarised in Figure 10.1 which should be read alongside Figure 10.2, setting out the growth-dependent planning paradigm. Together they describe a richer and more balanced planning system that can operate more effectively across different local social and economic circumstances.

In making this argument it should be noted that it is not claimed that the planning system alone can generate the conditions for

Figure 10.1: Planning beyond growth dependence

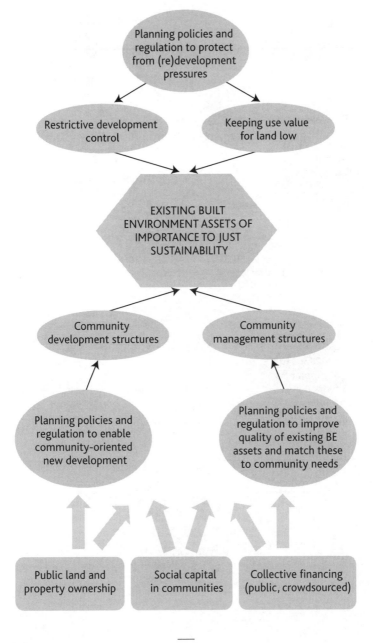

Figure 10.2: Growth-dependent planning

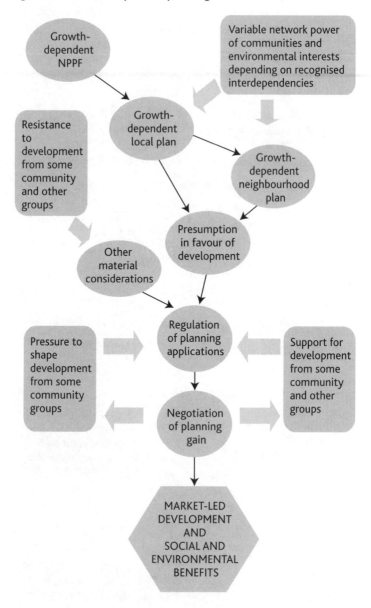

well-being and just sustainability. There is clearly a need for other forms of government action, some of which have been touched on in the above discussion. A functioning welfare state and accessible health service, together with a revived council housing programme, all have a vital role to play in supporting the needs of low-income households and maintaining their well-being. Effective and fair regulation of health and safety standards for housing and of environmental regulation with regard to pollution and contamination are also essential. But the planning system can play a role, particularly where the shaping of the urban environment is concerned. It is these aspects that the remainder of this chapter addresses.

There are two key principles involved in a reformed planning system. First, planners, together with local communities, need to identify whether, in any particular locational context at any particular time, growth-dependent planning is an appropriate mode of planning to be adopted. This involves asking the key questions in Box 10.1.

> **Box 10.1: Guiding questions for considering the relevance of growth-dependent planning**
> - Are the economic conditions right for this mode to be effective?
> - What are the social and environmental benefits that will be generated?
> - Will these be equitably distributed?
> - And does the proposed development, together with the negotiated planning gain, command the support of the local communities?

The growth-dependent paradigm does have some potential to enhance community well-being by creating new environments with housing of a good standard, well-designed green spaces and infrastructure, provision for active mobility and mitigation of environmental risks. This would produce more areas within towns and cities that promote well-being and could also, through planning gain, provide benefits for surrounding areas, say, in terms of green space improvements or even changes to local mobility patterns. However, despite these positive aspects, growth-dependent planning is limited in two respects. First, improvements in the urban environment will be dependent on the scale of new development. This will be constrained by economic circumstances. Even during booms, while it may generate significant amelioration of the experience of living in a locality, such development could only affect a proportion of urban households. Second, the households that will benefit from the new environments are likely to be from higher rather than lower-income groups, given the market dynamics underpinning such development. The spillover benefits to lower-income communities are likely to be dependent on the negotiation of planning gain, which is also constrained by the market profitability of developments.

It is also the case that the growth-dependent approach works better for some aspects of this well-being and sustainability agenda than others. New housing will, of course, be of a higher standard than existing housing, particularly with regard to issues such as higher thermal efficiency, which have only relatively recently been a focus of building regulations. Green spaces can be incorporated within developments and these developments can be planned to incorporate sustainable urban drainage systems to avoid localised flooding. They can also be located so as to avoid pollution and flood risks, although this depends on developers bringing sites forward that are in such low-risk locations, and on the planning system resisting development on sites that are in higher-risk locations, even if the developers identify these as being locations of market demand for housing and other land uses.

The promotion of more active mobility and other means of reducing car dependence can be more difficult. Again, the location of a development with regard to existing public transport networks depends on the developer's landholdings and where the developer has been able to buy sites. Putting in a public transport infrastructure is likely to be too expensive for the majority of development projects. And while a development can promote itself as car-free – without car parking and with provision for bicycles in terms of storage and cycle paths – this has to fit within a broader network of public transport and cycle routes to be fully effective. In Freiburg, where car-free developments have been promoted, this works because of the comprehensive tram system that exists and is extended in line with the planning of new development sites (sites that are usually released through the mechanism of public landownership).

Recognising the limitations of the growth-dependent planning paradigm implies the second key principle of a reformed planning system. This is that there needs to be provision for an alternative form of planning beyond growth dependence. This would allow for alternative approaches that are not reliant on market-led development. Instead these approaches would use the resources of local communities – residential and business – to create ways of developing, enhancing and managing the environments of the locality. The principles guiding such planning would be an appreciation of the value of existing places and land uses, even if they are not valued highly by market dynamics. There would be an overriding aim of meeting the needs of existing communities, particularly lower-income communities, thereby contributing to sustainability under the banner of just sustainability. The key questions to be asked are set out in Box 10.2.

Box 10.2: Guiding questions for planning beyond growth dependence

- Are more vulnerable groups in the locality, those who already have a lesser share of society's benefits, losing out through the change that is occurring due to development and changes of use?
- Is the change that is occurring contributing to a pathway towards a more environmentally sustainable future for the locality?

This will involve a degree of asymmetry within the planning system, since it requires the needs and desires of lower-income communities and the just sustainability agenda to be prioritised. Under such reforms there would be a presumption in favour of proposals that met these needs and that could be argued to be in line with just sustainability aims. Such proposals would be favoured over and above market-led propositions, and accorded a degree of flexibility in their treatment by the planning system so that they could be progressed. In effect, in areas where growth-dependent planning was not considered to be appropriate, all the biases in the planning system towards market-led development would be reversed, creating biases towards well-being, justice and sustainability.

What is needed now is a view of planning as a system, a profession and a set of practices that offers and enables choice in different localities and at different times as to which approach will be most appropriate. This would give planners, local politicians and local communities the tools with which to tackle the challenges that face us in the 21st century. These are severe challenges, but there is scope for a positive and creative response, rather than slipping back into a lazy and probably ineffective reliance on facilitating market-led growth.

The parting words are left to philosopher John Gray, commenting on the insights of John Maynard Keynes:[7]

> We do not find ourselves today struggling with the aftermath of a catastrophic world war. Yet the situation in Europe poses risks that may be as great as they were in 1919.... Facing these dangers, Keynes's disciples insist that the only way forward is through governments stimulating the economy and returning it to growth.
>
> It is hard to imagine Keynes sharing such a simple-minded view. As he would surely recognise, the problem isn't just a deepening recession, however serious. We face a conjunction of three large events – the implosion of debt-based finance-capitalism that developed over the past twenty years or so, a fracturing of the euro resulting from fatal faults in its design, and the ongoing shift of economic power from the west to the fast-developing countries of the east and south....
>
> I suspect Keynes would be just as sceptical about the prospect of returning to growth. With our ageing population and overhang of debt, there's little prospect of developed societies keeping up with the rapid expansion that is going on in emerging countries. *Would we be better off thinking about how we can enjoy a good life in conditions of low growth?* (emphasis added)

Notes

Preface

[1] Rydin (2010a).
[2] See Jackson (2009).

one

[1] Work by the most significant theorists include Pierre and Peters (2000), Berir and Rhodes (2003) and Stoker (2003); a good edited collection is by Pierre (2000).
[2] See Stone (1989) for the source of this classic quote.
[3] The key proponent here is Bob Jessop; see, for example, Jessop (2008).
[4] Patsy Healey has done the most to develop this approach; see, for example, Healey (2006).
[5] Jürgen Habermas' work is extensive; a useful introduction is provided by Eriksen and Weigård (2003).
[6] The introduction to the second edition of *Collaborative planning* discusses this; see Healey (2006).
[7] See Innes and Booher (2010).
[8] A key paper providing such a critique is by Tewdwr-Jones and Allmendinger (1998).
[9] Lindblom (1977) remains a key reference on the potential for commercial organisations to exercise an investment strike; the concept was used in a planning context in Rydin (1986).
[10] Again see Tewdwr-Jones and Allmendinger (1998).
[11] See Rozee and Powell (2010).
[12] See Rydin (1999) for a review.
[13] See www.southwark.gov.uk/info/200152/section_106/796/current_project_bank_ideas
[14] Williams (2012) provides an excellent account of progress towards zero-carbon housing.
[15] See Innes and Booher (2010).
[16] Jean Hillier is the chief exponent of the agonistic perspective on planning; see, for example, Hillier (2002).
[17] The Adam Smith Institute specialises in this approach; see, for example, www.adamsmith.org/sites/default/files/research/files/ASI_Planninginafreesociety.pdf
[18] The Planners Network UK is currently exploring such an approach; see www.pnuk.org.uk

two

[1] Accounts of planning history can be found in Cullingworth (1999), Rydin (2003, Part 1) and Ward (2004).
[2] Ambrose and Colenutt (1975) remains the best and most accessible account of this period.

[3] See Hall (1980) for a readable discussion of *Great planning disasters*.

[4] Dunleavy (1981) covers this thoroughly.

[5] See Evans (1980, 2004), Cheshire and Sheppard (2004, 2005) and Cheshire (2005).

[6] See Rydin (1986).

[7] Allmendinger and Thomas (1998) discuss many aspects of planning in this period; Imrie and Thomas (1999) and Brownill (1990) cover Urban Development Corporations; see also Brindley et al (2006).

[8] See Crawford et al (2009) for a thorough account of climate change and planning policy.

[9] This sequential test was introduced (in effect but not in name) in the Planning Policy Guidance Note No 13 (PPG13) on transport and planning in 1994 and formerly established as central government policy in PPG6 on retailing and town centres in 1996.

[10] The Urban Task Force report of 2005 established this approach within government policy; see also Carmona et al (2010).

[11] See ODPM (2003).

[12] Barry Needham's book (2006) is a good discussion of this.

[13] The NPPF (DCLG, 2012a) is available at www.gov.uk/government/uploads/system/uploads/attachment_data/file/6077/2116950.pdf; the Welsh equivalent is available at http://wales.gov.uk/topics/planning/policy/ppw/?lang=en; the Scottish at www.scotland.gov.uk/Publications/2010/02/03132605/0; and the Northern Irish version in the form of a regional development strategy at www.planningni.gov.uk/index/policy/regional_dev.htm

[14] The NPSs are available from the Planning Inspectorate portal at http://infrastructure.planningportal.gov.uk/legislation-and-advice/national-policy-statements and the National Infrastructure Plan, including its various updates, from the Treasury site at www.hm-treasury.gov.uk/infrastructure_nip.htm

[15] See Rydin (1986).

[16] This is being recommended – with practice guidance – by the Local Housing Delivery Group, 'a cross-industry group involving a broad group of stakeholders with an interest in home building in England'; see www.local.gov.uk/web/guest/environment-planning-and-housing/-/journal_content/56/10171/3619786/ARTICLE-TEMPLATE

[17] See Gallent and Robinson (2012).

[18] See DCLG guidance (2007) available at www.gov.uk/government/uploads/system/uploads/attachment_data/file/11500/399267.pdf

[19] The *Enterprise Zone prospectus* (DCLG, 2011) is available at www.gov.uk/government/uploads/system/uploads/attachment_data/file/6274/1872724.pdf

[20] The Planning Inspectorate portal is available at: www.planningportal.gov.uk/planning/planninginspectorate

[21] Section 38 of the 2004 Planning and Compulsory Purchase Act states that decisions on planning applications 'must be made in accordance with the [development] plan unless other material considerations indicate otherwise.'

[22] The National Infrastructure Planning portal is available at http://infrastructure.planningportal.gov.uk

[23] See Gallent and Robinson (2012).

[24] See Innes and Booher (2010).

[25] See Rydin and Pennington (2000).

[26] See Gallent and Robinson (2012).

[27] See Lee et al (2013).

three

[1] See Oxley (2004) for an accessible introduction.

[2] The data for agricultural land values is from Knight Frank's England Farmland Index available at http://my.knightfrank.com/research-reports/english-farmland-index.aspx; the data for residential land values are from the Valuation Office Agency and available at www.homesandcommunities.co.uk/ourwork/residential-land-value-data

[3] The residual method is explained in all standard valuation texts such as Millington (2000) or Scarrett (1990).

[4] See Adams (2008).

[5] There is a large selection of environmental economics textbooks available exploring this argument; see, for example, Perman et al (2011).

[6] See above.

[7] Data for construction industry employment and output is available from: www.ons.gov.uk/ons/index.html

[8] This is discussed in Hague and Hague (2011).

[9] See above.

[10] See the project website for all details at www.elephantandcastle.org.uk/pages/home/0/elephant_castle.html

[11] The quote is from www.southwark.gov.uk/elephant

[12] See Kitchen (2007), particularly Chapters 2 and 3.

[13] There is a useful resource at www.PlanningResource.co.uk/go/cil_maps that maps proposed CIL rates; see also Monk and Burgess (2012), available at www.rics.org/uk/knowledge/research/research-reports/s106-to-cil-transition

[14] The data on local government finance is from *Local government financial statistics for England* (2012) available at www.gov.uk/government/uploads/system/uploads/attachment_data/file/7476/2158981.pdf

[15] Further details on City Deals are available at www.dpm.cabinetoffice.gov.uk/content/city-deals

[16] Details of the Heseltine review are available at: www.gov.uk/government/publications/no-stone-unturned-in-pursuit-of-growth

[17] Details of the New Homes Bonus are available at www.gov.uk/government/policies/increasing-the-number-of-available-homes/supporting-pages/new-homes-bonus

four

[1] Data on the share of manufacturing in the UK economy is for 2009 and taken from BIS (2010) available at www.bis.gov.uk/assets/BISCore/business-sectors/docs/m/10-1333-manufacturing-in-the-UK-an-economic-analysis-of-the-sector.pdf

[2] Nikolai Kondratiev was a Russian economist during the Stalin era who posited the existence of these cycles in his 1925 book, *The major economic cycles*. They were named Kondratiev waves by Joseph Schumpeter (see below).

[3] Joseph Schumpeter was an Austrian-American economist and political scientist who analysed capitalism in terms of waves of creative destruction in his 1943 book, *Capitalism, socialism and democracy*.

[4] David Harvey is a British geographer, now working in the US, who has written widely on urban issues from a Marxian perspective; the text that is probably most relevant here is his 1985 book, *The urbanization of capital*. His own website is at http://davidharvey.org and he tweets from @profdavidharvey.

[5] The World Bank data are for July 2012 and taken from www.bbc.co.uk/news/business-18815595

[6] The data and the following quotes are from Davis (2011).

[7] The data for these demographic statistics are drawn from the Office for National Statistics 2012 report available at www.google.co.uk/url?sa=t&rct=j&q=&esrc=s&source=web&cd=4&ved=0CDUQFjAD&url=http%3A%2F%2Fwww.ons.gov.uk%2Fons%2Frel%2Fpensions%2Fpension-trends%2Fchapter-2--population-change--2012-edition-%2Fbkd-pt2012ch2.pdf&ei=xJZyUI6IHKi_0QXCkYDICA&usg=AFQjCNFmH_C7LcENJkLja7gI97qXuygKVg

[8] For example, see Bloom et al (2011) available at www.nber.org/papers/w16705 or www.hsph.harvard.edu/pgda/WorkingPapers/2011/PGDA_WP_64.pdf

[9] See Thornley (2012) for the development of this argument.

[10] See House of Commons (2008).

[11] See Goodley and Bowers (2012).

[12] See Sillett (2013).

[13] See Garfield et al (2013).

five

[1] See Rydin (2010b); this covers much of the material in this section.

[2] There are many publications on ecological modernisation; for example, see Murphy and Gouldson (2000), Mol and Sonnenfeld (2000b), Young (2000), Mol and Sonnenfeld (2000a, 2000b), Lundqvist (2004) and Barrett (2005).

[3] The above tend to focus on the national level; for a discussion of the concept at a lower scale, see Gibbs (2000, 2003).

[4] The Zero Carbon Hub provides a portal on matters relating to zero-carbon housing at www.zerocarbonhub.org; the discussion on non-residential development is less well advanced.

[5] See Zero Carbon Hub (2011) available at www.zerocarbonhub.org/resourcefiles/Allowable_Solutions_for_Tomorrows_New_Homes_2011.pdf

[6] See Haskins (2007) and Domenech (2009).

[7] See DCLG (2012a).

[8] Information about the BRE Innovation Park is available at www.bre.co.uk/innovationpark; information can also be found from the Alliance for Sustainable Building Products at www.asbp.org.uk/members

[9] See Fountain (2012), available at www.nytimes.com/interactive/2012/06/05/science/0605-timber.html. See also Bridport House, Shoreditch: www.karakusevic-carson.com/2012/bridport-house-hackney

[10] See www.eyeswideopen.com.

[11] See Sturgis and Roberts (2010).

[12] The classic text is von Weizsäcker et al (1998); this spawned a wealth of activity under the banners of 'Factor Four', 'Factor Ten', and so on, which can be readily revealed by an internet search.

[13] See the Foresight report on sustainable energy management and the built environment, GOS (2008). The following quote is from p 59 and the relevant footnote is no 58.

[14] See work by Patrick Devine-Wright and Simon Guy such as Guy and Shove (2000), Guy (2006), Devine-Wright (2007) and Devine-Wright and Clayton (2010).

[15] See DCLG (2012a).

[16] These are reviewed in Rydin (2010b); see also Williams (2012).

[17] There is a wealth of material on 'gentrification'. Some representative references are Zukin (1987), Smith (1996), Hamnett (1991) and Lees (2000), with a useful compilation in Lees et al (2008).

[18] Guidance on the rules governing planning gain can be found through the Planning Portal at www.planningportal.gov.uk/planning/applications/decisionmaking/ conditionsandobligations; current best practice guidance is available at www.gov. uk/government/publications/planning-obligations-practice-guidance

[19] Full details of this research on child poverty, including the report and a searchable map, are available at www.endchildpoverty.org.uk/why-end-child-poverty/ poverty-in-your-area

[20] The quote is from 'The gap between many rich and poor regions widened because of the recession', *The Economist*, 10 March 2011 (www.economist.com/ node/18332880?story_id=18332880).

[21] The papers discussed are Buckner and Escott (2009), Loftman and Nevin (1995) and Atkinson (2004).

[22] See www.neweconomics.org/press/entry/buying-local-worth-400-per-cent-more for more details, with the interactive tool available at www.neweconomics. org/projects/plugging-leaks

[23] See Oxley (2004) for an introduction to the concept of environmental externality.

[24] See Walker (2012) for an excellent review of the environmental justice concept.

[25] See Walker (2012, p 67) on how this kind of planning logic reinforces environmental injustice.

six

[1] See Jackson (2009).

[2] Richard Layard's ideas are fully expressed in the Lionel Robbins Lectures 2003-03, available at http://stoa.org.uk/topics/happiness/Happiness%20-%20Has%20 Social%20Science%20A%20Clue.pdf; the specific points is made in Lecture 1, p 15.

[3] See Jackson (2009, pp 40-2).

[4] This point is made in Lecture 2; see Note 2 above.

[5] Kuznets (1962).

[6] This quote is widely available, for example, at www.utne.com/realizing-the-vision/ real-change-is-up-to-us.aspx

[7] Details of the Genuine Progress Index are available at http://rprogress.org/ sustainability_indicators/genuine_progress_indicator.htm

[8] Details of The World Bank's genuine savings rate initiative are at http://web. worldbank.org/WBSITE/EXTERNAL/TOPICS/ENVIRONMENT/EXTEE I/0,,contentMDK:20502388~menuPK:1187778~pagePK:148956~piPK:216618 ~theSitePK:408050,00.html. The latter indicator has also been critiqued – see, for example, Pillarisetti (2005).

[9] The website for the Happy Planet Index is at www.happyplanetindex.org; see NEF (2012) for their measuring well-being initiative.

[10] See Asheim (2000).

[11] The UK National Well-being website is at www.ons.gov.uk/ons/guide-method/ user-guidance/well-being/index.html

[12] See Wilkinson and Pickett (2010).

[13] A portal to the resources of Michael Marmot's work on health inequalities is available at www.instituteofhealthequity.org

[14] See Marmot Review (2010), available at www.instituteofhealthequity.org/projects/fair-society-healthy-lives-the-marmot-review

[15] See Walker (2012).

[16] See Agyeman (2013).

[17] The need for the Thames Tideway Tunnel is due to the dominant paradigm of water-based sewerage systems and the combined nature of the existing drains dealing with storm water and sewage; further information is available at www.thameswater.co.uk/about-us/10115.htm

[18] The EUGRIS portal on soil and water management in Europe provides this data at www.eugris.info/FurtherDescription.asp?Ca=1&Cy=1&DocID=C&DocTitle=Statistics_and_related&T=United%20Kingdom&e=456

[19] The British Geological Survey (www.bgs.ac.uk) is the key resource here.

[20] The UK Climate Impacts Programme (UKCIP) provides a range of resources addressing the environmental hazards associated with climate change at www.ukcip.org.uk

[21] See Crawford et al (2009).

[22] Data from Department for Transport at www.gov.uk/government/uploads/system/uploads/attachment_data/file/3085/41.pdf

[23] Data is taken from the summary of government statistics in the Friends of the Earth briefing on road transport, air pollution and health available at www.foe.co.uk/resource/briefings/road_air_pollution_health.pdf

[24] Data is from the RAC Foundation, available at www.racfoundation.org/assets/rac_foundation/content/downloadables/road%20accident%20casualty%20comparisons%20-%20box%20-%20110511.pdf

[25] See GOS (2007).

[26] There is a valuable database on housing statistics available through Shelter at http://england.shelter.org.uk/professional_resources/housing_databank

[27] See Pickard and Parker (2013).

[28] See www.gov.uk/government/organisations/department-for-communities-and-local-government/series/english-housing-survey

[29] See DECC (2012a), available at www.gov.uk/government/uploads/system/uploads/attachment_data/file/66017/5272-fuel-poverty-monitoring-indicators-2012.pdf

[30] See Rydin et al (2012).

[31] A comprehensive review is provided by Tzoulas et al (2007); see also Rydin et al (2012).

[32] See Ulrich (1984), Hartig et al (1991) and Wolf and Flora (2010).

[33] See www.rspb.org.uk/Images/everychildoutdoors_tcm9-259689.pdf (p 6).

[34] See Wolf and Flora (2010).

[35] See Pugh et al (2012).

[36] See Gill et al (2007).

[37] See Wrigley (2002), Beaulac et al (2009) and Agyeman (2013).

seven

[1] Oxley (2004) provides a good introduction to the workings of the housing market.

[2] See Crook and Whitehead (2002) and Whitehead (2007); the definition of this term has varied with central government policy so that, at the time of the Livingstone mayoralty, it included categories such as key worker housing as well as housing provided by housing associations; it is now also used to cover lower-than-market-price housing for sale.

[3] See Montague (2012); details of the Montague Review are available at www.gov.uk/government/news/montague-plan-offers-boost-to-private-rented-sector

[4] See, for example, the advice and background at www.homesandcommunities.co.uk/ourwork/s106

[5] See Hall et al (1973).

[6] See Barker (2004); the Barker Review website is still available at www.barkerreview.org.uk

[7] See Rydin (1986).

[8] The amount that can be charged depends on the kind of tenancy: secured, assured or affordable housing; the details are explained at www.adviceguide.org.uk/england/housing_e/housing_renting_a_home_e/renting_from_a_social_housing_landlord.htm

[9] Details are available at http://england.shelter.org.uk/get_advice/housing_benefit_and_local_housing_allowance/changes_to_local_housing_allowance/housing_benefit_changes_2013; see also Stephens and Williams (2012).

[10] Details of the Right to Buy are available at www.gov.uk/right-to-buy-buying-your-council-home/overview; current information on the policy, including the use of receipts, is set out in DCLG (2012b), available at www.gov.uk/government/uploads/system/uploads/attachment_data/file/5937/2102589.pdf

[11] See Collinson (2012a).

[12] See Collinson (2012a, 2012b).

[13] The quote is from www.tcpa.org.uk/pages/garden-cities.html

[14] See www.tcpa.org.uk/pages/garden-cities.html

[15] See Hetherington (2012) and also www.letchworth.com/heritage-foundation

[16] See Williams (2012).

[17] See TCPA (2011).

[18] See www.cltfund.org.uk

[19] This is based on trusts listed at www.communitylandtrusts.org.uk

[20] The story of Coin Street is told in Brindley et al (2006).

[21] Colin Ward's *The hidden history of housing* is available online at www.historyandpolicy.org/papers/policy-paper-25.html

[22] Quote taken from http://thedabbler.co.uk/2011/06/plotlands

[23] See Ian Abley's online material at www.audacity.org/IA-05-04-09.htm

[24] See Note 21 above.

[25] See Pickerill and Maxey (2009, 2012).

[26] Data is from the Department for Communities and Local Government Housing and Construction statistics available at www.gov.uk/government/organisations/department-for-communities-and-local-government/series/house-building-statistics

[27] See the announcement at www.gov.uk/government/news/first-self-build-projects-to-benefit-from-multi-million-fund

[28] Details on Almere are available on the Self-build portal at www.selfbuildportal. org.uk/homeruskwartier-district-almere; the Baugruppen activities in Freiburg are covered in Little (2006).
[29] HM Government (2012).
[30] See WSBF (2011).
[31] The BRAC website is at www.brac.gov; see also the website for heritage consultant Celia Clark at www.celiaclark.co.uk/index.php?option=com_content&view=art icle&id=55&Itemid=37
[32] See Gallent and Bell (2000).
[33] See Note 21 above.

eight

[1] For details see www.planningportal.gov.uk/permission; the link to 'change of use' for business under 'Common projects' on the right goes to more information on the Use Classes Order.
[2] DCLG (2012a).
[3] See Smith (2012).
[4] See Ferm (forthcoming, 2014).
[5] See the Westminster City Council Core Strategy at www.westminster.gov.uk/ services/environment/planning/ldf/corestrategy
[6] See DECC (2012b) for a review of available measures.
[7] See Jones (2013).
[8] More details are available at www.marleyeternit.co.uk/Roofing/Concrete-Tiles/ EcoLogic-Ludlow-Major-Interlocking-Tile.aspx
[9] See Duncan (1974) and Donnison (1974).
[10] See Curran and Hamilton (2012).
[11] See Ellaway and Macintyre (2000), Robinson et al (2000) and Dowler and Caraher (2003).
[12] See Roger Tym and Partners (2000), available at www.nrpf.org.uk/PDF/ retailcapacity.pdf
[13] See CB Hillier Parker (2000), available at www.nrpf.org.uk/PDF/ secondaryshopping.pdf
[14] These are set out at www.nrpf.org.uk/PDF/summary.pdf
[15] See Kennedy (2012).
[16] Ziella Bryars' online material is available at http://wiki.emptyshopsnetwork. co.uk/index.php/W12_Shopping_Centre
[17] Details of this initiative are available at www.gov.uk/government/policies/ improving-high-streets-and-town-centres
[18] See Gonzalez and Waley (2012).
[19] See http://theteenagemarket.co.uk
[20] Aiesha (2010).
[21] See Ferm (forthcoming, 2014).
[22] See data from http://england.shelter.org.uk/professional_resources/housing_ databank
[23] Details of the Affordable Homes Programme are available at www. homesandcommunities.co.uk/affordable-homes
[24] See Griffiths (2010).
[25] Although note the pressure from the European Commission to increase the rate of VAT on energy-saving materials at www.building4change.com/page.jsp?id=1688

[26] See DCLG (2006), available at www.gov.uk/government/publications/empty-dwelling-management-orders-guidance-for-residential-property-owners

[27] See SQW Consulting (2010).

[28] More details are available at www.renewaustralia.org

[29] See Jackie Sadek's blog at www.estatesgazette.com/blogs/jackie-sadek/temorary-use

[30] For more details see www.meanwhile.org.uk

[31] More details are available at www.insidehousing.co.uk/closing-time-for-living-over-the-shop-project/1446809.article

[32] Sourced from www.davislangdon.com/upload/StaticFiles/EME%20Publications/Capital%20Allowances%20Technical%20Data/CA_TB09.pdf

nine

[1] See Dooling (2012) for a perspective on the homeless and parks.

[2] The quote is from Flint (2012, p 202).

[3] See GOS (2007).

[4] See Atkinson and Flint (2004).

[5] See Minton (2009).

[6] See Carrell (2012).

[7] See, for example, Kennelly (2011) on the experience of young people in relation to the Olympic Park development.

[8] Some of the examples below are drawn from McVeigh (2012).

[9] See Woodin et al (2010).

[10] See Pennington and Rydin (2000).

[11] There is a growing literature on community gardening and food growing; see Agyeman (2013), Eizenberg (2013) and the guide issued by Action with Communities in Rural England available at www.acre.org.uk/our-work/community-led-planning/News/New+Community+Food+Growing+Topic+Sheet

[12] See Johnston (2012).

[13] See the article in *The Guardian*, 28 June 2012, p 13.

[14] See the Pub is the Hub website at www.pubisthehub.org.uk

[15] Rydin (2010a, p 63).

[16] Examples are in Hampstead (www.keatscommunitylibrary.org.uk), Friern Barnet (www.fbpeopleslibrary.co.uk) and Kensal Green (www.savekensalriselibrary.org – still at campaign stage).

[17] See http://suffolkreads.onesuffolk.net/news/new-chapter-for-suffolk-s-libraries

[18] See Aiken et al (2011).

[19] See http://atu.org.uk

[20] See above.

[21] See http://locality.org.uk/locality

[22] See above.

[23] See a review in Hielscher (2011) and a discussion in Seyfang and Haxeltine (2012); see also Jones (2012).

[24] See www.brightonenergy.org.uk and www.bristolenergy.coop

[25] See http://spacehive.com

[26] See www.prsc.org.uk and www.gasworksdock.org.uk

[27] See Kaszynksa et al (2012).

[28] The original paper is Hardin (1968), and is widely available online.

²⁹ See, for example, Pennington (2000).

³⁰ The Nobel prize winner has a prolific output, but see Ostrom (1994) and Ostrom et al (1990).

³¹ The literature on social capital is extensive, but useful reviews of the concept that are relevant to the urban planning context are provided by Kearns (2003), Rydin and Holman (2004), Middleton et al (2005) and Dale and Newman (2010).

³² Gallent and Robinson (2012).

ten

¹ See DCLG (2012a).

² This quote can be found on the US EPA website at www.epa.gov/environmentaljustice

³ Details of the Aarhus Convention can be found at http://ec.europa.eu/environment/aarhus

⁴ For details on the Greater London Authority Low Emissions Zone see www.london.gov.uk/priorities/transport/green-transport/low-emission-zone-delivering-cleaner-air-in-london

⁵ Gallent and Robinson (2012).

⁶ See, for example, Wates (2000), Hamdi (2010) and Roseland (2012), all of which are excellent.

⁷ Gray (2012).

References

Adams, D. (2008) *Greenfields, brownfields and housing development*, London: Wiley Books.

Agyeman, J. (2013) *Introducing just sustainabilities: Policy, planning and practice*, London: Zed Books.

Aiesha, R. (2010) 'Planning for markets: understanding the role of planning policy and management approaches in sustaining markets in London', MPhil thesis, Bartlett School of Planning, University College London.

Aiken, M., Cairns, B., Taylor, M. and Moran, R. (2011) *Community organisations controlling assets: A better understanding*, York: Joseph Rowntree Foundation.

Allmendinger, P. and Thomas, H. (1998) *Urban planning and the British New Right*, London: Routledge.

Ambrose, P. and Colenutt, B. (1975) *The property machine*, Harmondsworth: Penguin.

Asheim, G. (2000) 'Green national income accounting: why and how?', *Environment and Development Economics*, vol 5, pp 25-48.

Atkinson, R. (2004) 'The evidence of the impact of gentrification: New lessons for the urban renaissance?', *European Journal of Housing Policy*, vol 4, no 1, pp 107-31.

Atkinson, R. and Flint, J. (2004) 'Fortress UK? Gated communities, the spatial revolt of the elites and time–space trajectories of segregation', *Housing Studies*, vol 19, no 6, pp 875-92.

Barker, K. (2004) *Review of housing supply: Delivering stability: Securing our future housing needs*, London: Office of the Deputy Prime Minister.

Barrett, B.F. (2005) *Ecological modernization and Japan*, London: Routledge.

Beaulac, J., Kristjansson, E. and Cummins, S. (2009) 'A systematic review of food deserts, 1966-2007', *Prevention of Chronic Diseases*, vol 6, no 3, p A105.

Bevir, M. and Rhodes, R. (2003) *Interpreting British governance*, London: Routledge.

BIS (Department of Business, Innovation and Science) (2010) *Manufacturing in the UK: An economic analysis of the sector*, BIS Economics Paper No 10A, London: BIS.

Bloom, D., Canning, D. and Fink, G. (2011) *Implications of population aging for economic growth*, PGDA (Program on the Global Demography of Aging) Working Paper No 64, Cambridge, MA: Harvard University.

Brindley, T., Rydin, Y. and Stoker, G. (2006) *Remaking planning: The politics of urban change* (2nd edn), London: Routledge.

Brownill, S. (1990) *Developing London's Docklands: Another great planning disaster?*, London: PCP Press.

Buckner, L. and Escott, K. (2009) 'Jobs for communities: does local economic investment work?', *People, Place & Policy Online*, vol 3, no 3, pp 157-70.

Carmona, M., Heath, T., Tiesdell, S. and Oc, T. (2010) *Public places – urban spaces* (2nd edn), London: Architectural Press.

Carrell, S. (2012) 'Park becomes battleground in fight to preserve communal land', *The Guardian*, 13 June, p 11.

CB Hillier Parker (2000) *Secondary shopping: Town centre dynamics: A research scoping paper*, London: National Retail Planning Forum.

Cheshire, P. (2005) 'Unpriced regulatory risk and the competition of rules: Unconsidered implications of land use planning', *Journal of Property Research*, vol 22, nos 2-3, pp 225-44.

Cheshire, P. and Sheppard, S. (2004) 'Land markets and land market regulation: progress towards understanding', *Regional Science and Urban Economics*, vol 34, no 6, pp 619-37.

Cheshire, P. and Sheppard, S. (2005) 'The introduction of price signals into land use planning decision-making: A proposal', *Urban Studies*, vol 42, no 4, pp 647-63.

Collinson, P. (2012a) 'So this home is "affordable"?', *The Guardian Money Section*, 23 June.

Collinson, P. (2012b) 'Rent controls: should they be brought back?', *The Guardian*, 1 June.

Crawford, J., Davoudi, S. and Mehmood, A. (2009) *Planning for climate change: Strategies for mitigation and adaptation for spatial planners*, London: Earthscan.

Crook, T. and Whitehead, C. (2002) 'Social housing and planning gain: is this an appropriate way of providing affordable housing?', *Environment and Planning A*, vol 34, no 7, pp 1259-79.

Cullingworth, J.B. (ed) (1999) *British planning: 50 years of urban and regional policy*, London: Athlone.

Curran, W. and Hamilton, T. (2012) 'Just green enough: contesting environmental gentrification in Greenpoint, Brooklyn', *Local Environment*, vol 17, no 9, pp 1027-42.

Dale, A. and Newman, L. (2010) 'Social capital: a necessary and sufficient condition for sustainable community development?', *Community Development Journal*, vol 45, no 1, pp 5-12.

Davis, E. (2011) *Made in Britain: Why our economy is more successful than you think*, London: Little Brown.

DCLG (Department for Communities and Local Government) (2006) *Empty dwelling management orders: Guidance for residential property owners*, London: DCLG.

DCLG (2007) *Strategic housing land availability assessments: Practice guidance*, London: DCLG.

DCLG (2010) *New policy document for planning obligations: Consultation*, London: DCLG.

DCLG (2011) *Enterprise Zone prospectus,* London: DCLG.

DCLG (2012a) *National Planning Policy Framework*, London: DCLG.

DCLG (2012b) *Reinvigorating Right to Buy and -ne-for-one Replacement: Information for local authorities*, London: DCLG.

DECC (Department of Energy and Climate Change) (2012a) *Fuel poverty monitoring indicators 2012: Annex to the annual report on fuel poverty statistics*, London: DECC.

DECC (2012b) *Improving energy efficiency in buildings: Resources guide for local authorities*, London: DECC.

Devine-Wright, P. (2007) 'Energy citizen: psychological aspects of evolution in sustainable energy technologies', in J. Murphy (ed) *Governing technology for sustainability*, London: Earthscan, pp 63-86.

Devine-Wright, P. and Clayton, S. (2010) 'Introduction to the special issue: Place, identity and environmental behaviour', *Journal of Environmental Psychology*, vol 30, no 3, pp 267-70.

Domenech, T. (2009) 'The role of industrial symbiosis in sustainable development', *The International Journal of Environmental, Cultural, Economic and Social Sustainability*, vol 5, no 3, pp 173-88.

Donnison, D. (1974) 'Policies for priority areas', *Journal of Social Policy*, vol 3, pp 12735.

Dooling, S. (2012) 'Urban ecological accounting: a new calculus for planning urban parks in the era of sustainability', in J. Flint and M. Raco (eds) *The future of sustainable cities: Critical reflections*, Bristol: The Policy Press, pp 179-201.

Dowler, E. and Caraher, M. (2003) 'Local food projects: The new philanthropy?', *The Political Quarterly*, vol 74, no 1, pp 57-65.

Duncan, S. (1974) 'Cosmetic planning or social engineering? Improvement grants and improvement areas in Huddersfield', *Area*, vol 6, no 4, pp 259-71.

Dunleavy, P. (1981) *The politics of mass housing in Britain, 1945-1975: A study of corporate power and professional influence in the welfare state*, Oxford: Oxford University Press.

Eizenberg, E. (2013) *From the ground up: Community gardens in New York City and the politics of spatial transformation*, Farnham: Ashgate Publishing.

Ellaway, A. and Macintyre, S. (2000) 'Shopping for food in socially contrasting localities', *British Food Journal*, vol 102, no 1, pp 52-9.

Eriksen, E.O. and Weigård, J. (2003) *Understanding Habermas: Communicative action and deliberative democracy*, London: Continuum.

Evans, A. (1980) *Rabbit hutches on postage stamps: Economics, planning and development in the 1990s*, Cambridge: Granta Editions.

Evans, A. (2004) *Economics and land use planning*, Oxford: Blackwell Publishing.

Ferm, J. (forthcoming, 2014) 'Delivering affordable workspace: Perspectives of developers and workspace providers in London', *Progress in Planning*.

Flint, J. (2012) 'Neighbourhood sustainability: residents' perceptions and perspectives', in J. Flint and M. Raco (eds) *The future of sustainable cities: Critical reflections*, Bristol: The Policy Press, pp 203-23.

Fountain, H. (2012) 'Structures of wood, taller and greener', *The New York Times Supplement, Observer*, 24 June, p 6.

Gallent, N. and Bell, P. (2000) 'Planning exceptions in rural England: Past, present and future', *Planning Practice & Research*, vol 15, no 4, pp 375-84.

Gallent, N. and Robinson, S. (2012) *Neighbourhood planning: Communities, networks and governance*, Bristol: The Policy Press.

Garfield, D., Greenhalgh, L. and Ogun, M. (2013) *Budget briefing*, London: Local Government Information Unit.

Gibbs, D. (2000) 'Ecological modernisation, regional economic development and regional development agencies', *Geoforum*, vol 31, no 1, pp 9–19.

Gibbs, D. (2003) 'Ecological modernisation and local economic development: the growth of eco-industrial development initiatives', *International Journal of Environment and Sustainable Development*, vol 2, no 3, pp 1-17.

Gill, S.E., Handley, J.F., Ennos, A.R. and Pauleit, S. (2007) 'Adapting cities for climate change: The role of the green infrastructure', *Built Environment*, vol 33, no 1, pp 115-33.

Gonzalez, S. and Waley, P. (2012) 'Traditional retail markets: the new gentrification frontier?', *Antipode*, published online 10 September.

Goodley, S. and Bowers, S. (2012) 'Effect of Olympics on house prices has been vastly overinflated', *The Guardian*, 16 June, p 33.

GOS (Government Office for Science) (2007) *Tackling obesities: Future choices* (2nd edn), London: Department for Innovation, Universities and Skills.

GOS (2008) *Powering our lives: Sustainable energy management and the built environment*, London: Department for Business, Innovation and Skills.

Gray, J. (2012) 'A point of view', *BBC News Magazine*, 22 July.

Griffiths, I. (2010) 'Half a million houses are lying empty, *Guardian* research shows', *Guardian Online*, 4 April.

Guy, S. (2006) 'Designing urban knowledge: competing perspectives on energy and buildings', *Environment and Planning C: Government and Policy*, vol 24, pp 645-59.

Guy, S. and Shove, E. (2000) *A sociology of energy, buildings and the environment: Constructing knowledge, designing practice*, London: Routledge.

Hague, C. and Hague, E. (2011) *Regional and local economic development*, London: Palgrave.

Hall, P. (1980) *Great planning disasters*, London: Weidenfeld & Nicholson.

Hall, P., Gracey, H., Drewett, R. and Thomas, R. (1973) *The containment of urban England*, London: Allen & Unwin.

Hamdi, N. (2010) *The placemaker's guide to building community*, London: Earthscan.

Hamnett, C. (1991) 'The blind men and the elephant: The explanation of gentrification', *Transactions of the Institute of British Geographers*, vol 16, no 2, pp 173-89.

Hardin, G. (1968) 'The tragedy of the commons', *Science*, vol 162, no 3859, pp 1243-8.

Hartig, T., Mang, M. and Evans, G.W. (1991) 'Restorative effects of natural environment experience', *Environment and Behavior*, vol 23, pp 3-26.

Harvey, D. (1985) *The urbanization of capital*, Oxford: Blackwell Publishers.

Haskins, C. (2007) 'A systems engineering framework for eco-industrial park formation', *Systems Engineering*, vol 10, pp 83-97.

Healey, P. (2006) *Collaborative planning: Shaping places in fragmented societies* (2nd edn), London: Palgrave.

Hetherington, P. (2012) 'A model community', *The Guardian*, 4 April, p 39.

Hielscher, S. (2011) *Community energy in the UK: A review of the research literature* (www.grassroots.org).

HM Government (2012) *The state of the estate in 2011*, London: HM Government.

Hillier, J. (2002) *Shadows of power: An allegory of prudence in land-use planning*, London: Routledge.

House of Commons (2008) *Public accounts: Fourteenth report*, London: Public Accounts Committee, Houses of Parliament.

Howard, E. (2010 [1898]) *To-morrow: A peaceful path to real reform*, Cambridge: Cambridge University Press.

Imrie, R. and Thomas, H. (1999) *British urban policy: An evaluation of the Urban Development Corporations*, London: Sage Publications.

Innes, J.E. and Booher, D.E. (2010) *Planning with complexity: An introduction to collaborative rationality for public policy*, London: Routledge.

Jackson, T. (2009) *Prosperity without growth: Economics for a finite planet*, London: Earthscan.

Jessop, B. (2008) *State power*, Cambridge: Polity Press.

Johnston, B. (2012) 'Report: help councils provide sites for local food', *Planning*, 18 May, p 8.

Jones, A. (2013) *Policy briefing: Protecting low-income households from reducing carbon emissions*, London: Local Government Information Unit.

Jones, R. (2012) 'Have you got money to burn?', *The Guardian Money Section*, 23 June.

Kaszynska, P., Parkinson, J. and Fox, W. (2012) *Rethinking neighbourhood planning: From consultation to collaboration*, London: ResPublica with the Royal Institute of British Architects.

Kearns, A. (2003) 'Social capital, regeneration and urban policy', in R. Imrie and M. Raco (eds) *Urban renaissance? New Labour, community and urban policy*, Bristol: The Policy Press, pp 37-60.

Kennedy, M. (2012) 'It's like a village again… Gritty east London get a smart new look', *The Guardian*, 23 June.

Kennelly, J. (2011) 'Sanitizing public space in Olympic host cities: The spatial experiences of marginalized youth in 2010 Vancouver and 2012 London', *Sociology*, vol 45, no 5, pp 765-81.

Kitchen, T. (2007) *Skills for planning practice*, London: Palgrave.

Kondratiev, N. (1925) *The major economic cycles* (in Russian), Moscow [publisher unknown]; trs. G. Daniels and published as (1984) *The long wave cycle*, New York, NY: Richardson & Snyder.

Kuznets, S. (1962) 'The new republic', 20 October, in C. Cobb, T. Halstead and J. Rowe (1995), 'If the GDP is up, why is America down', *The Atlantic Monthly October*, p 67.

Lee, M., Armeni, C., de Cendra, J., Chaytor, S., Lock, S., Maslin, M., Redgwell, C. and Rydin, Y. (2013) 'Public participation and climate change infrastructure', *Journal of Environmental Law*, published online 15 December.

Lees, L. (2000) 'A reappraisal of gentrification: towards a "geography of gentrification"', *Progress in Human Geography*, vol 24, no 3, pp 389-408.

Lees, L., Slater, T. and Wyly, E. (eds) (2008) *The Earthscan reader in gentrification*, London: Earthscan.

Lindblom, C.E. (1977) *Politics and markets*, New York: Basic Books.

Little, J. (2006) 'Lessons from Freiburg on creating a sustainable urban community', MArch dissertation (http://bergenokologiskelandsby. no/grupper/hus-og-energi/design-og-lokalsamfunn/baugruppe-essay-rev-270508-199.pdf).

Loftman, P. and Nevin, B. (1995) 'Prestige projects and urban regeneration in the 1980s and 1990s: a review of benefits and limitations', *Planning Practice and Research*, vol 10, nos 3-4, pp 299-316.

Lundqvist, L. (2004) *Sweden and ecological governance: Straddling the fence*, Manchester: Manchester University Press.

McVeigh, T. (2012) 'Free food, sharing and caring: the spirit of community is reborn in the Yorkshire hills', *Observer*, 6 May, p 17.

Marmot Review (2010) *Fair society, healthy lives*, London: Department of Health.

Middleton, A., Murie, A. and Groves, R. (2005) 'Social capital and neighbourhoods that work', *Urban Studies*, vol 42, no 10, pp 1711-38.

Millington, A.F. (2000) *An introduction to property valuation* (5th edn), London: EG Books.

Minton, A. (2009) *Ground control: Fear and happiness in the twenty-first-century city*, London: Penguin Books.

Mol, A.P.J. and Sonnenfeld, D.A. (2000a) 'Ecological modernisation around the world: An introduction', *Environmental Politics*, vol 9, no 1, pp 1-14.

Mol, A.P.J. and Sonnenfeld, D.A. (2000b) *Ecological modernisation around the world: Perspectives and critical debates*, London: Frank Cass.

Monk, S. and Burgess, G. (2012) *Capturing planning gain – The transition from Section 106 to the Community Infrastructure Levy*, London: Royal Institution of Chartered Surveyors.

Montague, A. (2012) *Review of the barriers to institutional investment in private rented homes*, London: Department for Communities and Local Government.

Murphy, J. and Gouldson, A. (2000) 'Environmental policy and industrial innovation: integrating environment and economy through ecological modernisation', *Geoforum*, vol 31, no 1, pp 33–44.

Needham, B. (2006) *Planning, law and economics: The rules we make for using land*, London: Routledge.

NEF (New Economics Foundation) (2012) *Measuring well-being: A guide for practitioners*, London: NEF.

ODPM (Office of the Deputy Prime Minister) (2003) *Sustainable communities: Building for the future*, London: ODPM.

ONS (Office for National Statistics) (2012) *Pension trends – Chapter 2: Population change*, London: ONS.

Ostrom, E. (1994) *Rules, games and common-pool resources*, Ann Arbor, MI: University of Michigan Press.

Ostrom, E., Gardner, R. and Walker, J. (1990) *Governing the commons: The evolution of institutions for collective action*, Cambridge: Cambridge University Press.

Oxley, M. (2004) *Economics, planning and housing*, London: Palgrave.

Pennington, M. (2000) *Planning and the political market: Public choice and the politics of government failure*, London: Athlone Press.

Pennington, M. and Rydin, Y. (2000) 'Researching social capital in local environmental policy contexts', *Policy & Politics*, vol 28, no 2, pp 33-49.

Perman, R., Ma, Y., Common, M., Maddison, D. and Mcgilvray, J. (2011) *Natural resource and environmental economics* (4th edn), London: Pearson.

Pickard, J. and Parker, G. (2013) 'Coalition plans push to revive housing', *Financial Times*, 4 March.

Pickerill, J. and Maxey, L. (2009) 'Geographies of sustainability: Low impact developments and radical spaces of innovation', *Geography Compass*, vol 3, no 4, pp 1515-39.

Pickerill, J. and Maxey, L. (2012), 'Low impact development: Radical housing solutions from the grassroots', in A. Davies (ed) *Enterprising communities: Grassroots sustainability innovations*, Dublin: Emerald Group Publishing Limited, pp 65-83.

Pierre, J. (ed) (2000) *Debating governance: Authority, steering, and democracy*, Oxford: Oxford University Press.

Pierre, J. and Peters, B.G. (2000) *Governance, politics and the state*, London: Macmillan.

Pillarisetti, J.R. (2005) 'The World Bank's "genuine savings" measure and sustainability', *Ecological Economics*, vol 55, no 4, pp 599-609.

Pugh, T., MacKenzie, A.R., Whyatt, J.D. and Hewitt, C.N. (2012) 'Effectiveness of green infrastructure for improvement of air quality in urban street canyons', *Environmental Science and Technology*, vol 46, no 14, pp 7692-9.

Robinson, N., Caraher, M. and Lang, T. (2000) 'Access to shops: the views of low-income shoppers', *Health Education Journal*, vol 59, no 2, pp 121-36.

Roger Tym and Partners (2000) *Secondary shopping: Retail capacity and need: A scoping paper*, London: National Retail Planning Forum.

Roseland, M. (2012) *Toward sustainable communities: Solutions for citizens and their governments* (4th edn), Gabriola Island, BC: New Society Publishers.

Rozee, L. and Powell, K. (2010) *Mediation in planning*, London and Bristol: National Planning Forum and the Planning Inspectorate.

Rydin, Y. (1986) *Housing land policy*, Farnham: Ashgate Publishing.

Rydin, Y. (1999) 'Public participation in planning', in B. Cullingworth (ed) *British planning: 50 years of urban and regional policy*, London: Athlone Press, pp 184-97.

Rydin, Y. (2003) *Urban and environmental planning* (2nd edn), London: Palgrave.

Rydin, Y. (2010a) *The purpose of planning*, Bristol: The Policy Press.

Rydin, Y. (2010b) *Governing for sustainable urban development*, London: Earthscan.

Rydin, Y. and Holman, N. (2004) 'Re-evaluating the contribution of social capital in achieving sustainable development', *Local Environment*, vol 9, no 2, pp 117-33.

Rydin Y. and Pennington, M. (2000) 'Public participation and local environmental planning: the collective action problem and the potential of social capital', *Local Environment*, vol 5, no 2, pp 153-69.

Rydin, Y. et al (2012) 'Shaping cities for health: complexity and the planning of urban environments in the 21st century', *The Lancet*, vol 379, no 9831, pp 2079-108.

Scarrett, D. (1990) *Property valuation: The five methods*, London: Taylor & Francis.

Schumpeter, J. (1943) *Capitalism, socialism and democracy*, London: G. Allen & Unwin.

Seyfang, G. and Haxeltine, A. (2012) 'Growing grassroots innovations: exploring the role of community-based social movements in sustainable energy transitions', *Environment and Planning C*, vol 3, no 3, pp 381-400.

Sillett, J. (2013) *Policy briefing: Managing budgeting in government: Public Accounts Committee report*, London: Local Government Information Unit.

Smith, L. (2012) *Planning reform proposals: House of Commons Library Standard Note SN/SC/6418*, London: House of Commons.

Smith, N. (1996) *The new urban frontier: Gentrification and the revanchist city*, London: Routledge.

SQW Consulting (2010) *Meanwhile use: Business case and learning points*, Cambridge: SQW (www.meanwhile.org.uk/useful-info/misc/SQW%20-%20Meanwhile%20Use%20Report%20May%2010.pdf).

Stephens, M. and Williams, P. (2012) *Tackling housing market volatility in the UK: A progress report*, York: Joseph Rowntree Trust.

Stoker, G. (2003) *Transforming local governance: From Thatcherism to New Labour*, Basingstoke: Palgrave Macmillan.

Stone, C. (1989) *Regime politics: Governing Atlanta, 1946-1988*, St Lawrence, KS: University of Kansas Press.

Sturgis, S. and Roberts, G. (2010) *Redefining zero: Carbon profiling as a solution to whole life carbon emission measurement in buildings*, London: RICS Research.

TCPA (Town and Country Planning Association) (2011) *Re-imagining Garden Cities for the 21st century: Benefits and lessons in bringing forward comprehensively planned new communities*, London: TCPA.

Tewdwr-Jones, M. and Allmendinger, P. (1998) 'Deconstructing communicative rationality: a critique of Habermasian collaborative planning', *Environment and Planning A*, vol 30, pp 1975-90.

Thornley, A. (2012) 'The 2012 London Olympics: what legacy?', *Journal of Policy Research in Tourism, Leisure and Events*, vol 4, no 2, pp 206-10.

Tzoulas, K., Korpela, K., Venn, S., Yli-Pelkonen, V., Kaźmierczak, A., Niemela, J. and James, P. (2007) 'Promoting ecosystem and human health in urban areas using green infrastructure: A literature review', *Landscape and Urban Planning*, vol 81, no 3, pp 167-78.

Ulrich, R.S. (1984) 'View through a window may influence recovery from surgery', *Science*, vol 224, pp 420-1.

Urban Task Force (2005) *Towards a strong urban renaissance: An independent report by members of the Urban Task Force chaired by Lord Rogers of Riverside*, London: Urban Task Force.

von Weizsäcker, E., Lovins, A.B. and Hunter Lovins, L. (1998) *Factor Four: Doubling wealth – Halving resource use*, London: Earthscan.

Walker, G. (2012) *Environmental justice: Concepts, evidence and politics*, London: Routledge.

Ward, S. (2004) *Planning and urban change*, London: Sage Publications.

Wates, N. (2000) *The community planning handbook: How people can shape their cities, towns and villages in any part of the world*, London: Earthscan.

Whitehead, C. (2007) 'Planning policies and affordable housing: England as a successful case study?', *Housing Studies*, vol 22, no 1, pp 25-44.

Williams, J. (2012) *Zero-carbon homes: A road map*, London: Earthscan.

Wilkinson, R. and Pickett, K. (2010) *The spirit level: Why equality is better for everyone*, London: Penguin Publishers.

Wolf, K.L. and Flora, K. (2010) *Mental health and function – A literature review*, Seattle, WA: College of the Environment, University of Washington (http://depts.washington.edu/hhwb/Thm_Mental.html).

Woodin, T., Crook, D. and Carpentier, V. (2010) *Community and mutual ownership: A historical overview*, York: Joseph Rowntree Foundation.

Wrigley, N. (2002) '"Food deserts" in British cities: Policy context and research priorities', *Urban Studies*, vol 39, no 11, pp 2029-40.

WSBF (Westminster Sustainable Business Forum) (2011) *Leaner and greener: Delivering effective estate management*, London: WSBF.

Young, S.C. (ed) (2000) *The emergence of ecological modernization: Integrating the environment and the economy?*, London: Routledge.

Zero Carbon Hub (2011) *Allowable solutions for tomorrow's new homes: Towards a workable framework*, London: Zero Carbon Hub.

Zukin, S. (1987) 'Gentrification: Culture and capital in the urban core', *Annual Review of Sociology*, vol 13, pp 129-47.

Index